A NEW EXPANDED EDITION OF THE BEST-SELLER

Teach Only Love

THE TWELVE PRINCIPLES OF ATTITUDINAL HEALING

A NEW EXPANDED EDITION OF THE BEST-SELLER

Teach Only Love

THE TWELVE PRINCIPLES OF ATTITUDINAL HEALING

GERALD G. JAMPOLSKY, M.D.

BEYOND WORDS Publishing INC

Beyond Words Publishing, Inc.
20827 N.W. Cornell Road, Suite 500
Hillsboro, Oregon 97124-9808
503-531-8700
1-800-284-9673

Design: Principia Graphica
Composition: William H. Brunson Typography Services
Managing editor: Kathy Matthews
Proofreaders: Marvin Moore and Susan Swanson

Printed in Malaysia
Distributed to the book trade by Publishers Group West

Library of Congress Cataloging-in-Publication Data
Jampolsky, Gerald G., 1925–
   Teach only love: the twelve principles of attitudinal healing / Gerald G. Jampolsky.
     p. cm.
   ISBN 1-58270-033-8 (pbk.)
    1. Mental healing.   2. Attitude (Psychology).   3. Love.   I. Title.
RZ401 .J34   2000
615.8'9—dc21
                                            99-087651
                                              CIP

The corporate mission of Beyond Words Publishing, Inc.:
Inspire to Integrity

This book is dedicated to my dear friends Ted and Vada Stanley, for being there for me, and whose friendship, love, and support throughout the years continues to be cherished.

CONTENTS

ACKNOWLEDGMENTS

I wish to express my deepest gratitude to Gayle and Hugh Prather for all of their help with both editions of this book. And for her loving support, invaluable reflections, and because she is always there for me, I thank my wife, Diane Cirincione.

For their editorial assistance with the first edition, I wish to thank William Thetford, Jules Finegold, Mary Abney, and Patricia Hopkins.

I am very grateful to Judy Skutch Whitson and Robert Skutch of the Foundation for Inner Peace for their permission to quote from *A Course in Miracles*. The quotes are noted with asterisks. And, above all, I am grateful for the inspiration and influence of *A Course in Miracles* on this book. *A Course in Miracles* is published by the Foundation for Inner Peace, P.O. Box 598, Mill Valley, California 94942-0598.

AUTHOR'S NOTE

It has been twenty-four years since the first Center for Attitudinal Healing was established in Tiburon, California, and seventeen years since the first edition of *Teach Only Love* was published. What has happened in the ensuing years? For me personally, many miraculous events have occurred that were beyond my imagination twenty-four years ago.

The principles of Attitudinal Healing, and the stories in this book that demonstrate them, continue to stand on their own as a testament to the power of Attitudinal Healing, not only for those facing catastrophic illnesses, but for all aspects of our lives. However, since this book was first published, the original seven principles have been expanded to twelve, and these new principles will be discussed in this new edition. I have also added a section on death and dying as well as one about my perceptions of God.

The original Center in Tiburon continued to grow and finally had to move to a larger space in Sausalito, California—a vacant school building that has proven to be an ideal home for us. We now have over three hundred volunteers and one hundred facilitators for the more than twenty-nine different groups that meet each week. There is a large Home and Hospital Division with over one hundred volunteers, and our Center is also working in elementary and high schools where children and staff are utilizing these principles in their everyday lives.

Since 1982 we have been working with adults and children who have AIDS, as well as children whose parents have AIDS. We created a poster that is used internationally—a cartoon by Jack Keeler of a boy saying, "I have AIDS. Please hug me. I can't make you sick." We have loss and grief groups for both children and adults. The Center is also actively working in prisons.

My wife and I, often accompanied by members of our staff, have traveled to such places as Russia, Croatia, Argentina, Chile, Australia, New Zealand, and Hawaii to give workshops and to consult with hospitals and other facilities. With other centers, we have responded to disasters such as the Oklahoma City bombing, establishing support groups as well as loss and grief groups.

We have a large volunteer training program, not only for our own Center but also for other agencies. Almost half of the people who now come to our Center participate in our Person to Person program. These people do not have catastrophic illnesses, but they come to learn how to apply the Attitudinal Healing principles of love and forgiveness in their own lives. The Center also continues to offer three-day workshops on Attitudinal Healing throughout the year.

To my amazement there are now more than 150 Centers or groups all over the world, including such diverse places as Ghana, West Africa, New Zealand, Australia, the Netherlands, Belgium, Switzerland, Italy, Argentina, Brazil, Russia, Germany, Croatia, as well as many more. As with the Sausalito Center, all of their direct services are free.

There is now a separate organization, the Network for Attitudinal Healing, International, that serves as a bridge connecting the various autonomous Centers and as a source for the exchange of information and ideas. This organization also helps coordinate an international conference on Attitudinal Healing that is held every two years. It is located at the Sausalito Center.

At our Centers we do not believe it is our function to change people or "fix them up." We are all there for our own healing and to learn to let go of what blocks our experience of love and prevents us from having peace of mind. We believe that by first healing our own hearts and minds, we then bring healing to the world we see. It is our absolute conviction that the most important gift we can give another person is our own inner peace and unconditional love. We believe that it is through forgiveness that our self-imposed blocks to love are removed and that we achieve this peace.

Gerald Jampolsky, M.D.
December, 1999

INTRODUCTION

As we emerge from the birth canal, we enter the world desperately struggling for breath. Most of us travel through life continuing to struggle, feeling unloved and alone. All too often we are afraid—afraid of sickness and death; afraid of God; even afraid of continuing to live. Often we leave the world the same way we entered it—desperately struggling for breath.

I believe there is another way of looking at life that makes it possible for us to walk through this world in love, at peace and without fear. This other way requires no external battles, only that we heal ourselves. It is a process I call "attitudinal healing," because it is an internal and primarily mental process. Properly practiced, it will, I believe, allow all of us, regardless of our circumstances, to begin experiencing the joy and harmony that each instant contains and to start our journey on a path of love and hope.

The mind can be retrained. Within this fact lies our freedom. No matter how often we have misused it, the mind can be utilized in a way that is so positive that at first it is beyond anything we can imagine. However, before the mind is retrained, it seems to be nothing but tightly locked compartments. We sense our potential, but it is held behind "closed doors." As you will begin to see as we progress on our journey together, these blocks are really only attitudes in need of healing, and because they are attitudes that we alone have chosen, they can be altered. With each small change, another "door" springs open. At the beginning we feel trapped and unable to escape our limitations, but as each unhelpful attitude is put aside, we increasingly see that our mind was never meant to be compartmentalized. All our potential has always been at hand because our mind is whole. The only barriers to our happiness are self-imposed.

Our attitudes determine whether we experience peace or fear, freedom or limitation, and to a large extent, whether we are well or sick. Love, in its true meaning, is the attitude that this book is about. Love is total acceptance and total giving—with no boundaries and no exceptions. Love, being the only reality, cannot be transformed. It can only extend and expand. It unfolds endlessly and beautifully upon itself. Love sees everyone as blameless, for it recognizes the light within each one of us. Love is the complete absence of fear and the basis for all Attitudinal Healing.

If you want to escape from pain, depression, sorrow, and anxiety so that you may experience love, then we can be sure it is no accident that you and I have found each other through this book. If you are anything like me, when you look back over your life, you are probably astonished at how much of your precious time has been spent in fear and in demonstrating and teaching fear, rather than love. This book is about what many of us at the Center believe is our purpose for being here—to teach only love. I will be writing to you about the approach I am trying to apply more consistently in my own life. It is also the one on which I founded the Center for Attitudinal Healing. I will be telling you some of the ways that the children and adults who have come there have taught me and others love, and how you and I can avail ourselves of that love in any difficulty that may arise.

May the reading of this book assist you in teaching love so that it becomes the drumbeat of your life and the song that you sing in all that you do. And may teaching love awaken you to who you truly are and to the Love that is unending and eternal, a Love that continues to unfold and expand upon itself.

I wish for you a happy and peaceful reading.

One
Attitudinal Healing

- Is there another way of looking at the world that changes our experience of life?

- Is it possible to choose to let go of fear and conflict completely?

- Is it possible to heal our painful thoughts and attitudes about the past and to bring peace to ourselves and others?

- Is it possible to forgive everyone who we think has hurt us, and to forgive ourselves for our mistakes and for the shame we feel about the past?

- Can we truly know peace and happiness while living in a world that seems so chaotic and crazy?

- Can we remove all our self-imposed blocks to love and come to know and trust in who we really are?

- Can we simplify our lives by recognizing that there are only two emotions—love and fear?

Attitudinal Healing answers all these questions with an unqualified and enthusiastic Yes.

What Is Attitudinal Healing?

Attitudinal Healing is based on the belief that it is not people or external situations that cause us to be upset. Rather, what causes us conflict and distress are our thoughts, feelings, and attitudes about people and events. Attitudinal Healing is letting go of fear and our negative, hurtful thoughts from the past.

Attitudinal Healing allows us to correct our misperceptions and to remove the inner obstacles to peace. This begins with a willingness to find another way of looking at the world, at life, and at death; to have peace of mind as our only goal; and to make forgiveness our primary function. It is discovering the effect that holding on to our grievances, blaming others, and condemning ourselves has, so that we can choose to no longer find value in them.

Attitudinal Healing asserts that when we let go of fear, only love remains and that love is the answer to all of the problems we face in life. It is the recognition that our true reality never changes and that Love is all there is.

My cherished friend Judy Skutch Whitson suggested the term when we first began the Center in 1975.

Attitudinal Healing

• Defines health as inner peace.

• Defines healing as letting go of fear.

• Regards our primary identity as spiritual and affirms that each individual possesses a quality of being or an inner nature that is essentially loving and that this loving nature is shared by all human beings.

• States that love is the most important healing force in the world.

- Does not tell other people what to do but offers them choices.

- Emphasizes equality in every aspect of our lives and affirms that we are all student and teacher to each other.

- Recognizes that peace is our only goal.

- Emphasizes listening with empathy and without judgment or advice.

- Sets the goal of living a life focused on unconditional love.

Attitudinal Healing views the purpose of all communication as joining and regards happiness as a choice. It recognizes that we are all worthy of love and that happiness is our own responsibility as well as our natural state of being.

Attitudinal Healing acknowledges that our only function is forgiveness. Rather than making decisions based on the fearful past, it states that we can learn to make decisions by listening to the inner voice of love.

The Benefits of Attitudinal Healing

The twelve principles of Attitudinal Healing are spiritual principles that lead us to love and away from fear. I think of the application of these principles as "practical spirituality" that can be used in every aspect of our lives. There is not one area where they do not apply. As we learn to change our attitudes and change our minds, we change our lives.

Some of the possible benefits of Attitudinal Healing include

1. Experiencing ourselves as love.

2. Finding inner peace.

3. Finding happiness.

4. Letting go of fear.

5. Letting go of judgments.

6. Letting go of guilt.

7. Letting go of being a victim.

8. Letting go of our fear of death.

9. Letting go of unforgiving thoughts.

10. Letting go of pain.

11. Letting go of being right and making others wrong.

12. Letting go of blame.

13. Letting go of our fear of the past and future.

14. Letting go of being a faultfinder.

15. Letting go of withholding love from anyone, including ourselves.

16. Letting go of our need to assign guilt or innocence.

17. Letting go of complaining and listing our hurts.

18. Letting go of our fear of intimacy.

19. Becoming a love-finder.

20. Counting our blessings.

21. Focusing on love rather than on appearances.

22. Walking through life more lightly.

23. Laughing more.

24. Living in a consciousness of giving rather than getting.

25. Recognizing that there is something greater than ourselves.

The essence of Attitudinal Healing is learning to release all thoughts from our minds except love thoughts. It is correcting the misperception that we are separate from each other and that others are attacking us. It is relinquishing the need to analyze, interpret, and evaluate our relationships. Attitudinal Healing is simply seeing others as extending love or as being fearful and asking for love. It is letting go of fear and guilt and choosing to see everyone, including ourselves, as innocent. Attitudinal Healing occurs when we make the decision to teach only love.

Two
The Only Lesson Is Love

There is really only one lesson to learn. But it can be stated many ways. One of the ways that I personally find meaningful comes from *A Course in Miracles*.

*Teach only love, for that is what you are.**

This statement indicates both our goal and the means to achieve it. It tells us that our essence is love. And it tells us how to recognize this in any difficulty, large or small: give only love; teach only peace; and never turn to attack in any form for your safety. This statement is the first and overall principle of Attitudinal Healing.

I have lost sight of this truth many times in my life. Yet it is encouraging how the simple truth keeps reappearing until finally we no longer allow ourselves to doubt. After I was given *A Course in Miracles*, many of the things that I was beginning to believe might be true became much clearer. Prior to that time I had come to recognize certain "realities," but I had not put these tantalizing facts into a consistent whole. A *Course in Miracles* was first published in 1975 and over one-and-a-half

---

*This and all subsequent quotations from *A Course in Miracles* are reprinted by courtesy of The Foundation for Inner Peace, P.O. Box 598, Mill Valley, California 94942-0598.

million copies are in print. It is a self-taught course for those interested in spiritual transformation. It suggests that we make the peace of God our only goal and forgiveness our only function, as we learn to listen to the Voice of God tell us what to think, say and do. The following summary of what I had become aware of prior to my encounter with *A Course in Miracles* could be called my first glimmerings of the principles of Attitudinal Healing.

- When we are occupied with helping another person, we do not experience fear.

- Fear does not bring about positive change, and it is always a mistake to provoke fear in an attempt to help others.

- We cannot successfully hide our fears from children.

- The true contents of our minds are open to all, especially children, and on one level all minds are in communication.

- We are not confined to our bodies, and we are not limited by physical reality.

- The mind, through its will to live, can affect the course of an illness.

- A preoccupation with the past disturbs our present attitudes.

- We can always learn from any situation we are currently involved in, no matter how undesirable it may first appear.

· Our inner goals determine our experience. We are not a victim of the world.

· Love does exist.

I want to share with you some of the experiences that led me to these conclusions. By seeing specifically how I learned to apply the lessons of love, you will, I hope, be able to make similar connections in your own life. I believe that what life is allowing us to discover is how to transfer what we see clearly and simply in one part of our experience to those areas where fear still seems reasonable.

The Truth Repeats Itself

"Yesterday was awful; today is terrible; and tomorrow will be even worse." That is the way my family looked at life when I was a boy. I suspect there may also have been a little of this attitude around when you were growing up. From generation to generation, we have all been steeped in the belief that the past predicts the future and that a mature person of good judgment carefully considers the lessons of the past when laying his plans. But *A Course in Miracles* points out that the past has only one lesson to teach us:

This Instant is the only time there is.*

The belief that the past provides the true laws of life enters our minds in an even more subtle way than through our direct attempts to control what is to come. We constantly think about the future and expect it to be like the past. Our fantasies and idle thoughts attempt to project in the future what we remember having liked in the past and to see eliminated what was difficult and painful.

When we think in this way we are not looking ahead in a practical and reasonable manner, but we are merely making a mental state that is composed almost entirely of fear. We believe that the general turn of the events in our lives is not to be trusted, and so we view everyone and everything either as an enemy or at least as potentially dangerous. This attitude, in turn, makes us feel unworthy of love. It makes us feel guilty and helpless and ambiguous about everything. It results in our attempt to control reality, and so the only talents we develop are manipulative ones.

This, of course, is the very mistake I myself have made so often. I tried to present myself to the world in a way that was quite different from how I was feeling. Inside, I may have been scared about what was going to happen, but outside I wore the costume of a man who was in control and to be respected. As is true of anyone who wears a mask, I felt isolated and misunderstood.

When we do not feel loved or lovable, we usually make the mistake of trying to gain control over the external circumstances we believe are causing our unhappiness. Because this goal can only be fulfilled in the future, the present moment is devalued. Even a dismal future over which we have some control seems preferable to this moment. And happiness, which requires that our full attention be on the present, becomes fearful. If some degree of happiness should occur, anyone with this attitude would immediately become suspicious of it. Whenever we are afraid, we think we see value in keeping the present free of all love and enjoyment. Fear stimulates an unconscious desire to be unhappy in order that we may focus on, and control, the future.

With this attitude, I not only felt unloved but unworthy of love. I was unworthy because I felt guilty of some unnamed sin. And because of my fear that my sin would be punished, I believed I had to sacrifice love in order to ward off punishment. One does not need religious training to believe he or she has to suffer.

Most of us feel very alone in the particular way we make mistakes. We think our guilt is private. I thought I owned the biggest stockpile of guilt in the world, and consequently, calamity seemed always to lurk just around the corner. Life was an outside force against which my own wits and energies were pitted. Living, in the true sense of the word—with zest, peace, joy, and harmony—seemed possible only for others. Wearing a mask myself, I believed what other people's masks communicated: They could be happy; I could not.

This general attitude resulted in existing but not living. More often than not, I confused happiness with pain, for I only felt alive when I was in the midst of a crisis. Therefore, I precipitated crisis after crisis. Since happiness itself seemed out of reach, this was the only way I knew to experience life. And as these adversities kept assaulting me, this approach seemed more and more a simple necessity. After all, I was merely a victim.

For much of my life, I believed that this outlook came to me naturally. Because of the genes I had received from my parents and the environment in which I grew up, I had become, through no choice of my own, fearful and guilt-ridden. It did not occur to me that the choice between love and fear was mine to make instant by instant. There are many people who came from surroundings much worse than mine who have chosen not to get stuck in their pasts. I chose to buy into my parents' philosophy and accept the limitations of my environment.

It is now clear to me that each one of us determines the beliefs by which we live. We think we must identify with our past, but this is not so. There is an alternative. The world is not held together by our worrying about it. We can lead a life that is free of fear. Just as I am, you are the determiner of everything that happens to you. This fact should not make us feel guilty; it should instead provide freedom to be at peace.

This was made evident to me during my third month of internship. As part of the Navy's V-12 unit, I was sent to Stanford University Medical School and was released from the Navy a year later to continue my medical education. In medical school, nearly a third of the class experiences symptoms of whatever disease is being studied. Some even come down with it. I was especially afraid of tuberculosis and was convinced I would eventually contract it and die. As it turned out, during my intern year, one of my assignments was to the tuberculosis ward. I had a recurring fantasy that I would take one deep breath in the morning and not breathe for the rest of the day.

One night, I was called on ward emergency for a fifty-year-old alcoholic who had tuberculosis and cirrhosis of the liver. She was bleeding from her esophagus, had vomited blood, and was in shock. Her pulse was feeble and her blood pressure was not measurable. I siphoned the blood from her throat and gave her cardiac massage. That night something was wrong with the oxygen machine, so I had to give her mouth-to-mouth resuscitation, to which she responded favorably.

When I returned to my quarters and looked at myself in the mirror, my green surgical gown was a bloody mess. Suddenly, it occurred to me that not once during that hectic hour had I been afraid. It was a powerful lesson to realize that when I focused only on helping, I had no fear. There were other times during my assignment to that ward, when I would evaluate what I was getting or not getting, that I was immobilized with fear. The lesson was clear. When a person is concerned only with giving, there is no anxiety. Later in life, I discovered that often there is also no pain or sense of limitation.

Minds Communicate

I had another important learning experience that same year, taught to me by an eight-year-old boy named Billy. We can't hide our emotions from children, no matter how hard we try. Thoughts that hurt us cannot be concealed, but they can be changed. Here are two quotes from *A Course in Miracles* that throw light on this lesson:

> *I have said that you cannot change your mind by changing your behavior, but I have also said, and many times, that you can change your mind.**

Later, the *Course* adds:

> *When someone truly changes his mind, he has changed the most powerful device that was ever given him for change.**

This is true whether we think it is our behavior or another's that is the problem. The mistake I made in the following incident involving Billy was to attempt to change him rather than concern myself with my own inner healing. When the mind accepts healing, that improved state will of itself extend to all the other minds with which it is joined.

Billy not only had cerebral palsy but also a behavior problem. As a psychotherapist, I had been seeing him and his parents, but things had gotten worse. One day his parents expressed their disappointment to me. I began to feel resentment toward Billy for making me look bad. Either resentment or pride results when our goal is to change someone.

That night I read an article by Milton Erickson, the father of modern hypnosis in the United States. It described using hypnosis with children. Apparently, all that was necessary was to relax the child, give a few suggestions, and—presto!—behavior would change. Part of me had doubts about the method, yet another part was desperate enough to try it.

The next time I saw Billy, I had him sit on the hospital gurney and gave him suggestions that his eyes were getting heavier and heavier, that his eyes were closing because they were so heavy, and that he was lying down on the gurney. Imagine my surprise when he did everything I suggested. He was cooperating perfectly, something he had never done before. But suddenly he sat up. His eyes were closed but he leaned over and put his nose against mine and said in his thick-tongued, palsied speech, "Dr. Jampolsky, your eyes are getting heavier and heavier." Then he broke out laughing.

After I recovered from the shock, we had a good laugh together. Kids are great therapists because they have not had the kind of formal teaching that can sometimes interfere with our deep intuitive knowledge. They know what is going on in an adult's heart. Instinctively, they seem to recognize that there is nothing hidden or secret, and they usually see through any mask we wear.

An Attitude Can Heal

While completing my internship in Boston, I became fully aware of the influence that attitudes have on the body. This recognition was brought forcefully to mind by two patients under my care who had stomach cancer. Medical consultants from Boston, Harvard, and Tufts universities agreed that both men, about the same age, had similar degenerative conditions and that neither could be expected to live more than six months. One of the men died two weeks later. The other continued to live, was dismissed from the hospital, and was doing well at the time I completed my internship.

The first man appeared to have no reason to live. He believed that even if he recovered there would be no way to resolve his day-to-day problems. He seemed more afraid of living than of dying. Death may have been an escape for him. The man who did not die had a determination to live; in effect, he refused to become a statistic on an insurance probability curve. Somehow, some way, he was convinced he would get well and would be able to complete the plans for his life.

This incident made me realize the importance of the thoughts we think. The direction they take actually constitutes our will to live or die. It is important to understand, however, that whenever I speak of a change in thought, I am not calling you to battle. The means whereby we redirect the mind are identical to the nature of the new direction itself. Peacefully we return to peace. Gently we lean into gentleness.

If ever you find yourself unwilling to think the kind of thoughts that you believe this book calls for, please do not frighten yourself. It is a letting go of tension that is being recommended. If you will simply think what it pleases you to think, what rests and comforts you, you will be doing all I suggest. There is no rationale in trying to force a change in your state of mind. Simply take careful notice of what it is that makes you happy to think and what makes you unhappy, and your mind will make the necessary adjustments itself.

It is clear to most physicians that attitude can affect organic illness. They know that the will to live or die can change the course of an illness. They know this even though such an attitude cannot be put under a microscope, measured, weighed, or replicated. The truths of the mind defy the usual standards of science. The conditions and general atmosphere produced by our attitudes can be seen reflected not only in the extreme case of a life-threatening illness but in all aspects of our lives. This became clear to me after my first attempt to pass my boards in psychiatry and neurology.

Taking the boards requires two days of oral testing. Although I had studied hard, I made the mistake of deciding I would be the calmest, coolest person ever to take the exams. My central focus was on wearing this mask, and everyone, especially my professional associates, marveled at my composure. A month later, I learned I had failed. All my energy had gone into pretending to be in control, and this left little attention that could be directed to answering the questions properly. The following year, without this distracting pretense, I took the exams and passed.

Afterward I joined the staff as a Fellow at Langley Porter Institute in San Francisco. My work there involved seeing children who were schizophrenic. Most of these youngsters were unable to speak, and the work was difficult, but at least I did begin to sense one important fact: Words are irrelevant to what we teach and learn.

The *experience* of love and peace is the only thing of importance that is communicated. It is this attitude of the heart and not what is said between two people that does healing work in both directions. One party's accumulation of verbal knowledge is of little use to deep inner healing. It was not long after this that I began to observe something which indicated that, along with words, training and experience also are of questionable value.

It became apparent to me that some second-year medical students were often more proficient with their patients than were third-year residents. This assumption led me to a discussion with Ethel Vergin, who at that time was the administrative head of the outpatient department. She was a keen observer of the medical staff and had seen many medical students, residents, and consultants come and go during her more than fifteen years at the Institute. She confirmed my observation.

I began to wonder why this discrepancy existed. It occurred to me that attitudes might be the primary factor, so I began examining the personality and performance of each individual resident I worked with. My study confirmed that in the handling of difficult illnesses, third-year residents usually showed little or no superiority over those with less experience. For instance, third-year residents treating patients diagnosed as chronic schizophrenics learn from many consultants that treatment of this disease is tedious and frequently very slow. So, when these residents see a new patient with chronic schizophrenia, they have already incorporated the values and attitudes of the consultants into their own thinking. They begin the patient's treatment with the expectation that progress will be protracted and difficult. The patient in turn identifies with the resident's limited expectation, and this becomes the reality that both experience.

Second-year medical students, who have not been contaminated by the negative experiences of many medical consultants, are usually enthusiastic and optimistic about seeing their first psychiatric patients. The label given to the patient means little to them. They just know that one way or another they are going to help the patient and that progress will be made. The patient identifies with this positive expectation and often improves more rapidly than with a third-year resident.

In this situation, it is clearly one's attitude that is of paramount importance and not one's experience. In fact, experience in this example can even be viewed as a hindrance. This taught me never to decide in advance what is best for another person and not to consider any human being as simply a predetermined statistic.

Far more often than we realize, we see only the past in the people we encounter. But it is actually our past, rather than theirs, that we view as part of them. Consequently, we do not respond to them but only to our various preconceptions. The genuine desire to see others as they are this instant will go a long way toward purifying our attitudes. There would be very little to dislike in other people if we refused to bring to them all our own judgments and petty grievances. Our past experiences cannot tell us of present love. Remembering and seeing are not the same, and that is why memories are of little use to us in forming loving relationships.

Love Exists

As my personal search continued, I became interested in Kirlian photography, which some investigators think depicts the electrical energy that surrounds all physical bodies. My research in this area led to an unusual experience with the Indian guru, Swami "Baba" Muktananda, whom I had heard of but had never met. In 1974, I was invited to his Oakland ashram to take Kirlian photos of his hands.

There were many young people at the ashram when I arrived, and they seemed to idolize Baba. At that time in my life, I was very judgmental toward gurus. I quickly concluded that these young people were emotionally mixed-up and probably had father fixations. It seemed likely that they found the ashram a safe place to be because they were unable to function in the real world.

Soon after my arrival, I was seated in a room with twenty invited guests. Baba entered; we were introduced and conversed through an interpreter. I took some photographs, was brushed by him with a long peacock feather, and sat down. As I observed others, I realized I had done everything wrong. Everyone else knelt before speaking to him; everyone, except me, had brought him flowers, fruit, or some kind of gift.

My mind ran wild when I realized I had done everything wrong. Yet I also had the sudden and distinct impression that, although Baba was talking aloud to others, he was having a nonverbal conversation with me. It was as though our minds were joined. I sensed with certainty that when he was finished speaking with the others, he would approach me, touch my face, and something very dramatic would happen.

He finished speaking and started to leave the room, and I said to myself, "Wrong again, Jampolsky." Suddenly, he was standing in front of me with his interpreter. He touched me, and everyone else in the room became excited. I was led to a small room and told that I would be left alone for a short period and that I should spend the time meditating. I was still suspicious, but as there seemed nothing to lose, I went along with the suggestion.

Then I had one of the strangest and most amazing experiences in my life, an experience that resulted in a radical shift in my belief system. After sitting quietly for five minutes, my body began to quiver and shake in an indescribable manner. Beautiful colors appeared all around me, and it seemed as though I had stepped out of my body and was looking down at it. Part of me wondered if someone had slipped me an hallucinogenic drug or if I were going crazy.

I saw colors whose depth and brilliance were beyond anything I had ever imagined. I began to speak in tongues—a phenomenon I had heard about but discredited. A beautiful beam of light came into the room, and I decided at that moment to stop evaluating what was happening and simply be one with the experience, to join it completely.

That was the last thing I remember until Baba's interpreter began shaking me and apologizing profusely, saying they had forgotten they had left me in the room. I was still in the sitting position. Two and a half hours had slipped by. I was taken downstairs, where there were about two hundred people in front of Baba. Everyone made room for me, and he and I had a conversation. Someone took a picture of me that I still have. I look like a male Mona Lisa with eyes of light and a smile hiding a secret.

Baba suggested that I obtain a picture of his guru and meditate in front of it. I chose not to do this. I did pick up a small book in which all the things I had experienced were described.

Although I usually have a high energy level, for the next three months it was heightened and I required very little sleep. I was filled with an awareness of love unlike anything I had known before. The power of this experience made me want to take a new look at everything I was calling real, because I had glimpsed a reality that is not limited to the physical plane. This was an important step toward a complete reappraisal of my concepts about God and spirituality. Although I didn't know it at the time, this experience was to prepare me for my encounter with *A Course in Miracles* a year or so later. But in the meantime, I was still struggling.

Three
Help Is Already Here

In the last chapter, I talked about how truth keeps reappearing. I can remember a time when I was a boy of four of five, lying on the grass and looking at the flowers and the mountains and the sky, and suddenly I felt God very close to me. This was a moment when I had no doubt about spiritual reality. I also remember that at the end of the Sunday drives our family used to take, I would pretend to be asleep and my father would carry me in his arms into the house. At those times, I saw clearly that he loved me. We are loved by God and loved by others. These are two basic truths that have returned to my awareness. They are by no means obvious, nor was it clear to me at first that they are the same truth.

Nothing Need Be Done Before We Are Ready

My problems with God began early. As a child I had dyslexia and saw the word *God* as *dog*. My difficulties and confusion continued, but I did not think deeply about them until a close friend in high school was killed in an automobile accident. His death left me feeling not only depressed but angry and bitter as well. Where was God's fairness in all of this? "How can there be a just God," I asked myself, "if He would stand by and allow an innocent life to be snuffed out before it had a chance to begin?" My answer was to turn from thinking of God altogether. If the question came up as to God's existence, I took the position of either an atheist or an agnostic.

Very quickly my judgments hardened against people who went to church or synagogue or who turned to God in any way. I saw them as fearful and intellectually soft. A belief in eternal life seemed equally silly. I thought that it was a concept which only people facing death would reach for and that heaven was a fantasy for those who had made very little of themselves.

As I now look back, I think that without being completely aware of it, I was actually battling against what I thought were God's designs on my autonomy. I believed that I, Jerry Jampolsky, should be the sole director of my life. Only I could determine what was best for me and for the people in my life. I saw the will as an attribute of the mind and believed that each body held within it a separate mind. I believed that in order to fulfill my function in life, it was inevitable that I compete against other people's wills.

When I dared for a moment to think that there was a reality based on God's will, I was certain that it must be against me. If it operated unrestrained, it would surely prevent me from having the things that gave me pleasure. There were a few fleeting moments when I seemed to have a little willingness to let God be the director, but only as long as I thought there was a way to nudge God to do things my way. Above all else, I wanted to remain in control, and therefore the concept of God's will seemed very threatening.

As I mentioned earlier, what I conceived of as real was limited to the physical. And I thought that I, being only a small part of it, was very often a victim of the physical world. So this control that was so important to me was very limited indeed. Not once did it occur to me that God's will could be the part of me and everyone else which represents our deepest yearnings and most loving desires. Not once did I think that God's will and my true will were the same.

In most people's lives, no matter how strong their disbelief in God, there are brief moments when the darkness lifts and they experience a peace and joy that is not of this world. I remember one such incident when I was a third-year medical student. During that moment I knew there was a God. It was at night and I had just delivered my first baby on obstetrical service. The miracle of perfection and harmony that I experienced had to be greater than any one man's understanding. I was in awe: I knew there had to be a universal force, a miracle of love, beyond my comprehension. And I was part of that miracle, part of the whole. For that one moment, I saw that nothing in the universe was separate, that everything and everyone were joined.

Unfortunately, the feeling did not last long. That event became a cherished secret, and I went back to the books, trying to memorize, analyze, understand, and make deductions based on a physical reality. And again I became a nonbeliever.

As far as prayer was concerned, I simply had no use for it. I thought that people who prayed were full of fear and were unrealistic. They were afraid to figure things out for themselves. I wanted nothing to do with such people. It was only much later that I realized I was the one who was fearful.

In the years that followed the completion of my training, I established a successful private practice, received some prestigious appointments, and had a growing national reputation in several fields. However, I had also become an alcoholic. My marriage of twenty years ended in a painful divorce. I often felt like a jigsaw puzzle that had been thrown into the air and scattered into a thousand pieces. I began sampling almost everything that came my way, both physical and mental. I tried all the therapies and all the groups, but nothing seemed to work. I knew I badly needed help, but I couldn't see any avenue open to me that offered even a glimmer of hope. I was aware that some people turned to God in their desperation, but that was not for me.

Always Respond with Gentleness

I was still very much in this valley of depression when one spring day a close friend, Judy Skutch Whitson, called me long distance from a telephone booth and said she wanted me to read some unpublished material she had just received. It was a set of manuscripts entitled *A Course in Miracles*, and she promised to bring them with her when she flew out to see me. In those days, I thought of this woman as the kind of person who becomes overly enthusiastic about too many things, but I loved her dearly, and so to placate her, I agreed.

The course she handed me was contained in black thesis binders, and I began with a section that is now printed in pamphlet form under the title *Psychotherapy: Purpose, Process and Practice*. It was the best possible place for me to have begun. Anywhere else and I would have been so put off by the heavy use of Christian terminology that I wouldn't have read farther.

We ask for help and help is given. Often we do not recognize that other people's alcoholism, sexual betrayals, chronic illnesses, and alienating behavior are actually cries for help. But unquestionably God recognizes every plea no matter what form it takes, and God finds some way to give us as much help as we are willing to receive at that time.

My help came in the form of *A Course in Miracles*, but I want you to know that I did not recognize it. At first, I was reading only to fulfill an obligation. As I continued, I was amazed at what happened. On a deep level that I did not even know existed in me, there was an instant in which I experienced the complete recognition that I had found my path. Later I was shocked when I realized I had heard a voice within me saying, "Physician, heal thyself."

To my astonishment, I became totally immersed in the *Course* and found myself having periods of peace that I had not thought possible. A completely new life began to open up for me as I recognized that my purpose here on earth was only to experience God and to extend peace—in other words, to teach only love. I then began to relate the *Course* philosophy to both my personal and professional lives, and the artificial walls I had built up between the two began to dissolve.

About five months after I began reading the *Course*, a critical experience occurred. One Sunday night I had gone out to dinner with some friends from Carmel. I had drunk a lot, but no more than usual, and I did not consider myself drunk. I went to bed about midnight, and around 2 A.M. I was awakened by a voice. For an instant I thought I was hallucinating and that in the next second I would begin seeing purple elephants on the wall and end in delirium tremens. I was frightened and immediately sat up in bed. I heard it again. This time I knew it wasn't an external voice but an internal one. Then it came for the third time: "You are entering a new phase of healing. It is no longer necessary for you to drink."

I started to sweat. What was I going to hear next? But I heard nothing more, and after about two hours, I finally got back to sleep. When I awoke in the morning, I had completely repressed the memory of what had happened. I shaved, showered, and went off to work as usual.

I returned home about 6:30 P.M. and, per my customary routine, went straight for the Scotch bottle. However, as my hand began to reach for it, I heard the voice again: "This is a new phase of healing. It is no longer necessary for you to drink." My hand did not finish its journey. Surprisingly, in the days and months to come, I never missed drinking, never felt I was sacrificing, never thought I was being socially inadequate.

I believe that the purpose of God's guidance is to show us how to release our minds from fear so we may know peace and be truly kind and sensitive to others, which we cannot do when we are fear-dominated. Both "no" and "yes" must therefore be left to Love's guidance.

Within three months after hearing the voice, I lost thirty pounds, going from 192 to 162 pounds. Having the tailor take in all my clothes was a wonderful experience. It was as if I were confirming a miracle that part of me still doubted ever happened.

The Dr. Jekyll/Mr. Hyde existence I had led—in which I had one personality in my office and another outside—began to dissolve. It became apparent that the only way to find true peace was to live a unified life. Every aspect of myself had to be included.

Unless we see the importance of consistency in everything we think, say, and do, our progress will be very slow. If our goal has not yet become to respond in gentleness to each call for help, we will also think that help is often withheld from us when we are crying out for it. Whenever we give help, we unfailingly see that the answer to all our needs is already within the very situation we think is hurting us. By becoming completely open and harmless, we see that there is no one who cannot help us and no instant when we are not surrounded by God's love and guiding presence.

Four
Heal Thyself

All minds are joined. Therefore, all healing can be looked at as self-healing. Our inner peace will of itself pass to others once we accept it for ourselves. All healing is inner healing, because love cannot be hindered by what appears to be separate or external. Giving to another mind is giving to our own. All correction is mental, and the strength of every mind is ours. The voice of love and oneness can always be heard. Love is our only function and destiny.

All Minds Are Joined in Love

Consider for a moment the concept that there is one all-uniting, universal Mind, one all-pervading Intelligence, and consider also its corollary, that there are no totally separate minds. One way this could be imagined is to think of the universe as an ocean. On its surface are waves. Yet the waves are made by and composed of ocean or water. If one wave should suddenly want to separate itself completely from the ocean, to accomplish this it would have to be wholly without water and without any connection with the movement of the ocean. How could it then roll and sparkle or in any way be like a wave? The simple fact is that a wave could not divide itself from the body of all waves and still remain a wave.

Here is another analogy. Once again, water will be our symbol for Mind. Imagine the universe as a vast pool of water, made up entirely of, and completely filled with, water. Now, scoop up a bucket of this water and pour it back in, and notice that the movement of part of the water affects every other particle of water in the universe. Notice also that the water which is poured back does not have to be aware of its effect on all the water in the universe in order to have its effect. It has its effect regardless.

Analogies prove nothing, of course, but it is not proof we are seeking. What we want is a broadening of our experience. Each of us is connected to all living things whether we are aware of this beautiful fact or not. Yet it is our unawareness of it that causes all our misery.

We have no private or unaffecting thoughts, *provided the thoughts we have are true or real*. If I, as a mind, am joined with all other minds, I have my influence on theirs whether or not I wish to. However, if I believe I can separate myself completely from Mind, I am simply self-deceived, for I could no more do this than a wave could separate itself from the ocean and still be a wave. And if a wave could somehow believe that it could accomplish this, that belief would not affect the perfect functioning of the ocean. Any thoughts or emotions I have which are based on the belief that I can cut myself off from Life will never affect Life. In other words, our negative ideas do not change reality, and this is the essential reason why all thoughts of guilt are as groundless as they are unhelpful. But it is also important to see that our fearful and destructive lines of thought do not contribute to our welfare or to the happiness and health of others. Very simply, what we think is either part of the problem or part of the answer.

There are thoughts that are true and thoughts that are mistaken. The thought of love, for example, is a light that can disperse thoughts of loneliness, illness, pain, and depression from our mind. On the other hand, the thoughts of guilt and fear can be very painful for us to entertain, but they cannot affect the peaceful core of our being, which is love.

Our body is a teaching machine. It will reflect on its screen the feelings and thoughts we program into it. The entry point for all programs is the mind, and what we see reflected throughout the body is what we have put into our mind. Our body will exhibit thoughts that are conflicted and anxious or ones that are peaceful, loving, and happy. It has no choice in this, but we do.

This concept can provoke guilt and confusion to the ego. It interprets this simple cause-and-effect relationship as just another opportunity to judge. "If I am sick," it reasons, "I am doing something wrong with my mind." But, of course, this is not entirely accurate. First, the ego is not questioning its own judgments, criticisms, and condemnations about what is going on in the body. Second, it is assuming that this self-censure is the remedy. And third, it believes that it is up to it alone to correct the focus of the mind.

Worrying about how we have been using our mind is merely a way of continuing to misuse it. Fear and regret are never a part of Attitudinal Healing, because they are a preoc- cupation with the past and not a loving, relaxing willingness to ask God for help right now. Warring with our thoughts is not the first step toward peace. Looking closely at our nega- tive thoughts and seeing that they do not represent what we wish to pursue, what we wish to be, and what we wish to extend to others is all the time and energy we need to spend on the ego. A mistake need only be seen as a mistake. Having seen it, we must now turn to our deeper, more central thoughts, which are thoughts of forgiveness, understanding, love, grati- tude, and peace.

The body reflects the contents of our mind. If our mind is peaceful, so is our body. But a peaceful state of mind cannot be forced, because force is not peaceful. Our mind connects with all other minds, and if our mind is peaceful, peace is the gift we pass along to others. Judging others for being sick or for having difficulties is not helpful to them or us. However, if our mind is full of attack thoughts, other minds do not automatically become a helpless victim of our attack.

The reason for this is that attack thoughts are based on the belief that other people's minds are separate in purpose and will from ours. When we judge others, we are merely attempting to convince ourselves that there can be an advantage to seeing some people as basically unlike us. This idle wish cannot affect reality, and so even though our attack thoughts do nothing to contribute to the comfort of our own bodies or to the ease and joy of others, they do not travel the universe creating havoc. They simply partake of, and are part of, what might be called the collective ego or the collective insanity. They are an utter waste of time and for that reason alone should be of no interest to us.

Inner Peace Passes to Others

Our ego—the fear part of our mind—wants conflict and separateness, which are the food for its survival. Peace and inner quiet are the mortal enemies of the ego. Peace comes from experiencing our unity with others. Love and peace are so interwoven that they can never be used separately. We will not have the experience of love encircling us until we have allowed peace within. Yet this peace has nothing whatsoever to do with our worldly circumstances.

I once heard a beautiful story that can help demonstrate this rule of Attitudinal Healing. There was a minister in Switzerland, sixty-four years old and near retirement, who began to question his life and his beliefs about God. As he did so, he started having many doubts about himself and his concepts of reality. He became so depressed that he decided to put God on the shelf and get a substitute minister. Attending the local pub became his major activity.

A few days after all these changes had begun, a message came from a woman in his parish saying that her husband had just died. She lived just two doors away, and the minister immediately went to her home. He knew exactly what to say because he had been in this situation many times before. However, just as he began to open his mouth, a little voice inside said, "Say nothing; just think the word *peace*." About five minutes went by, and as he started to give his talk again, he received the same message. An hour went by, and finally the wife began to speak. She said that she could not understand what was happening. Her husband was dead in bed and she was experiencing more peace than she had ever felt before in her life. He told her that he also was experiencing peace as never before. He felt for the first time that he knew what the peace of God was.

Let us remember each day, each minute, each second—and let us remember especially in the morning as we rise—that when we accept peace for ourselves, peace is received to some degree by all others. This is the way the world will be transformed, not by our attacking those who favor attack.

Bodily Conditions Cannot Block True Communication

We protect our sense of separateness in many ways. One that I run across frequently in my work is the belief that deep and meaningful communication with another is *already* blocked because of some bodily state or condition. The age of the body, physical damage to the brain, differences in ethnic or social backgrounds, autism, language barriers, and inebriation are just a few examples of differences between bodies that appear to keep minds divided. But none of these physical states are the barriers they seem, because actual communication and all the benefits that flow from it pass between our love center and the love center of other people. This true communication is completely unaffected by the education, training, age, or condition of our brains. I recognize that this statement is not an obvious truth to most. However, the consistent, straightforward practicing of love will bring all the evidence of its truth that could possibly be wanted, and after a time, all arguments that minds are not in communication will be seen as merely silly.

I would like to offer an account by Sharon Tennison, a registered nurse, who sometimes writes down her experiences and insights and shares them with me. Sharon's thoughts always beautifully illustrate the fact that we are joined, on a very deep level, and that bodily states of any type cannot impede real communication.

It's a mid-December day—Christmas presents already made or bought, my children busy for the evening—and I have nothing planned. I call one of the hospitals to see if they need help for the evening shift. As usual, they do.

Floating from hospital to hospital and working on any floor or intensive care unit can be an exciting adventure. One never knows what kind of medical, emotional, or spiritual crisis the next eight hours will bring or what personalities one will get to know by the end of the shift. On the way to a hospital, my heart usually finds itself putting out

a little prayer that I will be placed where I can be most useful or where I can learn something that my brain or soul
needs. Then the matter is dropped and I assume, wherever
the placement is, that is where I am supposed to be.

This particular night the assignment is on a medical
floor. During report from the off-going nurse, I learn about a
very irascible patient in room 322. He is a forty-four-year-
old man (my age) in end-stage alcoholic disease who gets
back at the world by all sorts of antisocial acts; the most
recent is refusal to ask for the bedpan, making it necessary
for the staff to be constantly changing linens. He is hostile
and combative and requires body and wrist restraints. The
day nurse is ready to be rid of him and I am not at all sure
about taking him on along with eight other sick patients.

I make the rounds of my rooms, and on approaching
room 322 a strong odor of formaldehyde floats through the
air. It becomes offensive as I enter the room. The curtains
are pulled tight around 322-B. I peek in, and there in the
bed is a shriveled little body rolled up in a fetal position
with blankets piled high, smelling for the world like one
of my anatomy or physiology lab experiments. I pull some of
the covers away from his face to get his attention, and he
doesn't appear to rouse. On my third attempt to rouse him,
he hurls verbal abuse, grabs his blanket, and again disappears under it.

I stand there looking at this little heap of humanity,
reflect on my own healthy body, and wonder how this can
happen to someone in forty-four years. That he is my own
age seems to impose a stronger bond between us in my heart.
How could this have happened?

I walk out and continue from room to room until I have
some idea about the rest of my patients. They are fairly

stable, emotionally in good places, with family members around for support and love. Only my little man in 322. I check with the desk—no, he never has visitors. On checking his drug cards, I see that he is receiving Paraldehyde 10 cc. intramuscularly every six hours for delirium tremens, and this is the reason for his offensive odor.

Dinner trays are brought at 5 p.m. I go to his room to see if he is able to feed himself. He doesn't even know the tray is there. Slowly my eyes adjust to the now-darkening room with the curtains still pulled tightly around the bed. I gently put a spoon of Jell-O to his mouth, and to my surprise he takes it in. Then another. And another. My mind is still puzzling and wondering if there is any way to reach this little withdrawn soul. My heart tells me that probably the only thing he would react to is just loving, gentle service. When he has had enough Jell-O, he pulls the cover up over his mouth and again disappears without a word. I remove his tray from the room and continue with the duties of the night.

At 6 P.M. it is time for his Paraldehyde. Five cc's in each buttock—a huge dose for the muscle to take—and I dread doing this to an already pained little man. I proceed to his room with the two syringes drawn full. As I enter, I realize that the formaldehyde smell is mixed with another. He has fought back at the world again—perhaps in the only way left to him, since his hands are restrained and his days numbered. Part of working with humanity at this level is for your senses to become dulled when necessary.

The room is now almost dark—a very faint night light is overhead—and I find myself standing there silently beside the curtained bed. Little remembrances start coming through my mind: words of Dr. Jerry Jampolsky, whom I had recently heard talking about "the most offensive people are *in the greatest need of love"; thoughts of "extending love," of "letting loose of the evaluator in myself," of "looking at this little man, really looking at him, and making him my brother." Knowing nothing else to do, I just let these thoughts be active in the space between us, almost a trancelike quiet. And something wells up in my heart, a different feeling, a realization, and somewhere deep inside me a knowing comes that perhaps this little man has never been touched in his entire forty-four years. Perhaps he was a poor little Mexican boy, the last one of a large family, born in some dusty, confused, frustrated place where migrant workers fight for survival. I could see a skinny little boy coming up in this world with no skills, no support, no love—and perhaps the bottle was the only consolation he had found in life. Was this little boy just in my mind or could it be one of those rare intuitions? I don't know or really care, because it does make me see into the possibility of my patient and feel a deep empathy that seems to well up from my very bones.*

I reach down to lift the black hair out of his eyes. He doesn't move. Again I put my hand to his forehead and clear more hair away. The least I could give to this little boy in my head is the touch that perhaps he never received before. Then, as I sit down on his bed, my heart simply takes over and my hands comfort in a simple kind of way. The mixed smells of the room have disappeared from my awareness and the syringes go patiently waiting.

There is a sense of being caught up in some place somewhere between the everyday and the heavenly planes, a place of the Now where nothing else matters except the moment. At some point, I hear myself saying to him in a voice more loving than my normal voice, "I know if you had another chance to live your life over, you wouldn't choose the bottle." It sounds like a strange thing to say once it is out, but it must have been the right thing. A hushed and sorrowful voice comes back: "Oh, no, ma'am"—so permeated with feeling and sadness. He then begins haltingly to tell me that he has been drinking since he was a teenager in El Paso, Texas. His has been a hard border-town life from the beginning. "I hate the taste. I drink to forget my misery." Somewhere in the conversation I ask if he thinks there is anything we can do to help him work with his addiction, and he tells me no, that it is like a monster. He knows he will go back to it if he lives this time to leave the hospital.

I consider that everything in my nursing skills is directed to helping people see their life problems, helping them gather the resources to begin to combat their limitations, offering the support and love and encouragement that makes them believe in themselves again—and yet this is not useful here. My heart just loves this little man. Whether he can quit alcohol or not is immaterial to me. He is precious, and by some quirk of fate, I have been allowed to see into him and love him somewhere deep where alcohol doesn't touch. And I share with him that I know what a battle life has been for him and that I understand if he can't quit—and it is OK— I find him a very special person and want to do anything I can for him to make him comfortable. By this time we are holding hands, and an incredible amount of feeling permeates the room.

I begin to become aware of another reality: the bed needs to be changed and the injections are over thirty minutes late. But what has happened is more important. I am sensing that this little soul may have to leave this crippled body, but he may go into eternity knowing that he has experienced love and acceptance.

As for me, I walk out of the room on my way to get fresh linens and hear myself exclaiming, "Oh, Jesus, this is how you must feel—about all the children of Earth—as we get caught in our webs of limitations and get lost. You see beyond all this into the core of our very being." So this is how unconditional love feels. It is my first experience at this depth, and I feel lifted into another dimension by being allowed to share in this oneness.

We untie this little man—no longer combative—and change his bed. He apologizes for the extra work. There is a new feeling in the room, and I have a fresh realization of how mountains of depression and frustration can be leveled through the extension of love.

When we begin to believe that our true identity is a spiritual being and that we are so much more than a body, our whole life begins to change. Seeing the essence of spirit and light in another person allows us to let go of our own bodily focus and recognize the same essence in ourselves. This profound transformation unites us in oneness with each other and with that which created us. Thus, true healing takes place in the heart, the mind and the soul. It is an act of unconditional love that does not focus on the deterioration of the body and allows us to experience joy and peace despite the condition of the body.

As I will stress many times in this book, within Attitudinal Healing the emphasis is on inner healing rather than outer healing.

Five

The Peaceful Preference

When I explain to people that the Center gives no treatment, one of the most common responses is, "Oh, I see, you help children adjust to pain and death." And this is indeed a reasonable assumption, but it is not Attitudinal Healing.

Attitudinal Healing recognizes a reality that is not connected to problems, upsets, or even life-changing tragedies. That reality is love. And love is entered and assimilated only as our mind loses interest in either fighting against or succumbing to the miseries of life. When the significance of this fact first begins to dawn on us, our initial reaction is likely to be one of confusion about how we should behave, because our tendency is always to want to know in what way truth is supposed to be applied to life. And of course the truth of love cannot be applied; it can only fill our heart. Once this is done, we will instinctively act in an appropriate way.

A center for children with catastrophic illness that does not have the goal of either healing the body or adjusting the mind to accept the illness is clearly not asking those who come to it to behave in any particular "way." Attitudinal Healing is not concerned with behavior, and this has occasionally been frustrating to some who have wished that we would take a stand either for or against a particular treatment, system, diet, or regime. Our "stand" is that all individuals have within them the resources to make those decisions for themselves, and we are there to help them and ourselves enter more deeply into that place of strength and understanding.

How then does a person who wishes to live in a more loving way go about making decisions? Attitudinal Healing addresses itself to this question by recognizing that *decisions are made by learning to listen to the preference for peace within us. There is no right or wrong behavior. But there is mistakenly motivated behavior. The only meaningful choice is between fear and love.*

There Must Be a Better Way

In this book, I have frequently pointed out that most decisions are made from fear and through judging the situation and consulting the past for what we need to change and how it should be changed. It is always the situation, or the people within it, that appears to need correction. If we are counseled to shift our concern from the outward picture to our own mental state, this requires a degree of trust that we are not in the habit of exercising. But surely it is obvious that if we continue running our lives strictly along the lines which our personal past dictates, nothing new can enter. By declining to judge—that is, choosing not to apply standards based solely on the past—we can look directly at what is happening and turn to this other reality within us, which is not attached to our old experiences, and receive a fresh insight. Our own very short history does not hold vast caches of wisdom. In fact, it is so personal in its bias and so distorted in how we now picture it that it is really of little use to us. I know of no story that better illustrates this point than that of Aeeshah Ababio. Here is an inspiring example of our capacity to turn from personal history toward the voice of happiness that can be heard within our heart.

Aeeshah has worked closely with all of us at the Center for several years. Her gifts of love and humor and her special insights have transformed many lives, young and old. And yet it was not very long ago that working this intimately with whites would have been unthinkable for her. Here is her account of how this major shift in her perception occurred.

Before I became a student of A Course in Miracles, *I was a Black Muslim and believed that only some of the people on earth were children of God. I felt it was necessary to separate myself from those who were ungodlike, and I had no idea that with this attitude I was limiting myself from experiencing the totality of God's presence. I believed that if God had wanted everyone to be brothers and experience brotherly love, He would have included all people in the African ethnicity.*

I had an enormous amount of love in my heart; however, it was only shared with a portion of the people on earth, and I added further to my confusion by teaching this lesson to others. I taught love and fear. I told my people that Whites were to be feared and hated because they were not children of God due to the color of their skin. As a result, my experiences with the people of this earth were mixed with love and fear, and I did not experience the totality of God's love. You may wonder how I came out of this confused state of mind. I did not do it alone. I was helped by my internal teacher, whom I now refer to as the Holy Spirit.

While on this path of spiritual confusion, I would experience moments in which I would sense an inner urge to know more and to be more than what had been shown me thus far. Books would come to me that were unrelated to my chosen path, but they spoke of another path which dealt with the concept of Oneness of God. These books stirred within me a longing that I was not fully capable of fulfilling. My desire to be at one with God was like a tiny light in a dark room, and I began to question my belief system. I wondered, "How could there be a Oneness of God if some are excluded?" The more I opened myself to experiencing this Oneness, the more I perceived within my chosen path a weakness that could not withstand the test of reason.

One day, in a moment of inner turmoil, I asked, "If there is a Oneness in God, how can I experience it?" No sooner had I asked than an answer began to come to me. It was a Sunday afternoon and I was reading the Tribune. On the front page was an article announcing a psychic seminar to be held at a nearby university. As I read, a voice from within me clearly told me that I was to attend this seminar. I was puzzled because I had never felt an inner voice. While I concentrated on what had transpired, again I heard, "Go."

The following morning I telephoned the institution where the seminar was to be held. I spoke with the secretary, who immediately referred me to the director of their program. I introduced myself and requested an appointment with him. He said he would be pleased to meet with me, and we made an appointment for the following afternoon.

I arrived a bit apprehensive about my reason for being there, and I went into the administrative office simply to get the appointment over with. The secretary informed me that the director was expecting me, and she took me into his office. I sat there wondering what this man thought of me. Did he think I was crazy because my dress code wasn't acceptable in the wider society? Did he wonder why this Black Muslim would come to see him? All kinds of thoughts ran across my mind. As I sat in a chair directly in front of *him, he was very patient as I fumbled through my purse to get the news clipping about the psychic seminar. He asked very quietly, "How may I help you?" I began talking nonstop about my chosen spiritual path and how I was guided to attend this conference, and I asked if it was possible for me to me to come. I added that I did not have any money and I knew that there was a fee to attend.*

He had listened very attentively, nodding his head as if he understood. Then he said, "You can attend, but you will have to agree to pay the fee at a later date." I agreed and left his office feeling a sense of accomplishment.

The following Sunday I found myself seated in a large auditorium filled with the people whom I had been taught to fear and hate because they were ungodlike. I moved forward to the front row so that the population I was in the midst of would not preoccupy my mind. I sat down and pulled my hat over my forehead so that my eyes would be shaded and folded my arms as a sign that I was to be on guard.

The day began with parapsychologists presenting information intended to bind the gap between psychology and spirituality. Their presentations were informative but dull. Finally, a lady named Judith Skutch came up, who was introducing a set of books entitled A Course in Miracles. *As she began to read the introduction, I again heard an inner voice, which said, "This is a tool for you, dear child. Use it and I will guide your way. For I am with you always." This lady began to glow, and again I was told, "This is your sister, whom I love dearly." I was filled with love in my heart for this lady. I also felt at home and safe. This was a very strange experience for me, because this lady was from among those people whom I believed were ungodlike. Yet a voice deep within me spoke of God's love for her. I sat quietly after her presentation, thinking about what had transpired. I no longer could base my separatist belief on anything I felt, because all I felt at that moment was unconditional love for all of the children of the earth. At that moment, God's love entered my heart and dispelled any false belief I had held about any of His children.*

It wasn't easy to sustain that transcended perception about my surroundings, and I began to feel doubt about my feeling of Oneness. I felt good inside, but I still wasn't sure if I should be experiencing love without measuring and evaluating. "Were these books necessary?" was a question that persisted in my consciousness. Why should I trust that one experience as a valid reason to purchase a set of books that I had never examined closely?

I sat in my seat for a prolonged period observing people moving toward the back of the auditorium, purchasing books from a man who was smiling and being very polite. I consciously felt that it would be a wild goose chase to buy these books with the idea that they would serve some useful purpose in my spiritual process. I looked at all the people in the auditorium and judged against them. Then I slowly walked to the back of the room and inquired about the cost. The man informed me in an unusually warm manner that they had sold all the books on hand. I felt relieved and thought this was a sign that I wasn't supposed to have them. Just as I was about to turn away, he said to me that his name was Jerry Jampolsky and that if I wanted them I could come to a meeting at his home on Thursday evening. He gave me the directions I would need. I left the seminar feeling very confused about my chosen spiritual path. I also felt a sense of being comforted by a still, small voice saying, "Be still, my child, and know that I am with you always."

At that time, my circle of friends and supporters con-sisted of others who were in the same thought system as myself. I wondered with whom I could possibly share this experience. How could I tell them that I wanted to go to the home of someone we felt must be avoided so that we would not be deceived? I knew I did not want to go alone, but I did want to go. As I pondered my situation, again, for only a moment, I heard a still voice saying, "Don't worry about who shall go, for that is already taken care of." I relaxed and made a choice not to rebuke this voice.

The next day a dear friend called to inquire about the psy-chic seminar. I shared with her my interest in A Course in Miracles *and said that I wanted to purchase these books, but I would have to go to Tiburon on Thursday evening. She was interested but unsure about going. I shared with her that I did not really want anyone else to know because we would have to be among people who were not children of God. When she heard that, she decided that she could not possibly let me go alone.*

I spent the rest of the week wrestling with my split mind. Was I crazy? Here I was wanting to go into the midst of beings whom I thought diabolical. Why was I going there? To get a set of books that a voice inside me insisted would guide me home. All of this did not really make any sense. But I knew that I would go.

On Thursday we arrived at Jerry Jampolsky's home, and he greeted us with a warm smile. Of course, I was suspicious of his warm regard for me. His home was filled with people, all of whom were classified by me as Satan's children. I saw myself as separate from everyone in the room except my friend; however, the room was very crowded and we were forced to separate. I found myself sitting quietly between two strange bodies that were unlike mine.

Once seated, our first instruction was to hold hands and sense our inherent connectedness. As I stretched forth my hands to the two people next to me, I closed my eyes to blot out the presence of their white bodies. My mind was active with fear thoughts—fears of the past, fears of oppression and racial strife. And fear that the children of God were connected and not separate.

I felt the grasp of their hands over mine. Then, as I began to breathe deeply, relaxing in the environment I was in, for a moment I began to feel loved and safe. And I was, to my surprise, sending love out to the people who were next to me and I could sense this loving energy moving out to everyone in that room. Again, I heard deep within me, "My child, teach only love, for this is what you are." I felt safe and at home. At that moment, I knew that everyone in that room was my brother and I was one with them. As I opened my eyes, these bodies whom I had perceived as enemies were transformed into friends and loved ones.

Aeesha later established a Center for Attitudinal Healing in Oakland, California, called the Oakland Connection. Among many other things that take place there, she and her husband, Kokomon Clottey, give workshops on racial healing. They have written a wonderful book—*Beyond Fear*—that is based on their concepts of racial healing and the principles of Attitudinal Healing. They also helped start a Center for Attitudinal Healing in Ghana, West Africa.

Peaceful Behavior Follows Peace

Consistent peace is not the same as regimented behavior. Our behavior should follow our peace of mind like a wake trailing the movements of a ship. If peace is our single aim in all we do, we will always know what to do because we will do whatever will protect and deepen our peace. This approach is in marked contrast to the exhausting attempt to decide every action beforehand on the basis of whether we think it will turn out right.

Our ego always wants to see its way clear before it acts. It prefers mental conflict now to simple action. It would rather pause and stew than move easily forward, and so it uses its favorite delaying tactic: the question of right and wrong.

We all want to be moral and good, at least in our own terms, and so the ego uses this desire to engage our attention in an interminable calculation of consequences. Yet it is only now that we can be good, kind, and gentle. No way exists in the present to accurately determine the future effect of the least of our actions. And it goes without saying that there is no way for us to go back in time and correct what we consider our past mistakes. No matter how long we try, we never know all the people our actions affect or whether the effect will be beneficial in the long run. Why then engage in an impossible task, no matter how well meaning it may seem, when genuine opportunities to be kind and truly helpful are all around us?

Understanding this releases us from a guilty preoccupation with the future and gives us permission to consult the present urgings of peace and love within our heart. Yet it must be stressed that, as we start out, this procedure will require trust. We must simply begin to do what our sense of peace indicates, even though we do not know the outcome. Of course, we never knew the outcome before, but we did have a certain sense of safety in thinking we had second-guessed the results. Now we admit that a loving preference is a more reliable basis for a decision than endless guesses about future consequences.

This concept became very real to me when I met Carol Chapman and her daughter, Hillary, who was hospitalized with a brain tumor at Children's Hospital in Los Angeles. Two weeks after our first meeting, I received a phone call from Carol. She reported that Hillary was going in and out of coma and that when her daughter was lucid she would beg to be taken off chemotherapy and x-ray treatment. Carol was deeply distressed and asked me what she should do. I told her that if she had asked me this kind of question a few years before I would have known exactly what to advise her. Now the only thing I knew to say to her was what I would tell myself: be still and listen to your inner voice and trust what you hear. I have learned that the only thing that can bring a restful assurance in an extreme and painful dilemma such as this is the voice of peace within us all.

My response did not satisfy her. She said she knew I was an expert in these matters and should therefore be able to give her a definite course of action. We talked a while longer, but she was still unhappy with me when we hung up.

The next day Carol called again, and this time her voice was quite serene. She told me that after we talked, she was able to quiet her mind and pray. And this, she said, was the answer she received: "There is no right or wrong. There is only love." The answer freed her mind from fear and allowed her to consult deeply her love for her daughter. What she then saw was that she wanted to stop all treatments as her daughter had requested.

Three weeks later, Hillary died a very peaceful death. Carol received the news at a conference where several other parents who had lost children to cancer were present, and they were able to comfort her in a way that only parents who have been through this could.

Once we realize that there truly is no right or wrong procedure, we can turn to love in complete confidence. But the peaceful preference that lies within our heart cannot be heard until we have relinquished our fearful desire for specific answers. First, we must recognize that any number of alternatives could be accompanied by the peace and love we desire. We see that we do not care personally which course of action we take but that we do care that our way be kind, harmless, and harmonious. Now our emphasis is on how we go, not where we go. And from this type of inner calm will always come a simple suggestion as to what to do. Our part is to gently trust this so that we can act from peace. And if a change or another course of action is needed later, we are not afraid to take it.

Instead of judging everything and trying to twist people and circumstances into appearances we like, the way of peace proceeds quietly and simply. Whenever life surprises us, our first reaction is now to consult that calm place within our heart. We stop and rest a moment in God's love. Then, if action is needed to restore our peace, we take the course that comes to us from our calmness. We act with assurance, for indeed we have been assured. And if later we need to ask again, we do so quickly and easily. Our purpose is not to seek peace in order to make rigid decisions or set for ourselves long-term rules but rather to make those decisions that will return us to peace this instant. For it is only when we are peaceful that we can be truly kind.

Six

The Twelve Principles of Attitudinal Healing

Shortly after I began working with *A Course in Miracles*, I was guided to begin a center where children with life-threatening diseases could come and help each other in an atmosphere of freedom and acceptance. As a doctor, I had been trained to believe that controlled, predictable progress could only occur on a vertical plane. Patients were in no position to help themselves because of their poor experience and limited knowledge. For them to attempt to assist other patients or to turn to them for help could be as dangerous as the blind leading the blind.

A Course in Miracles had presented me with another view, one that I had already begun to experience through the kinds of insights I told you about earlier. This view gave evidence of a different set of facts: That we have an internal physician, the voice of love. And that it can be heard when we recognize that it speaks not only in us but in the heart of everyone else, even the youngest child or the most unsophisticated and uneducated adult. We hear it by listening for it in others. Because it is love, it is in loving that we come to know it and trust it with every detail of our lives.

As a doctor, I had believed that gentleness and empathy were nice attributes to have but that it was not absolutely necessary for the practice of love and forgiveness and the practice of medicine to go hand in hand. Now I had come to realize that healing and love are inseparable, and I wanted our center to be a place where every attempt that individuals made to help themselves or someone else would be thoroughly gentle and completely kind.

I envisioned not so much an organization as an atmosphere of mutual trust. Here, the doctors, therapists, volunteers, and all the support people would come together with the children to learn from each other as equals, not to "teach" from a position of superiority. At our center we have implemented this concept with a kind of dress code for all our groups and activities: Everyone must remove his M.D., Ph.D., R.N., M.S.W., or any other credential before entering.

I knew that the Center had to be a supplement to the traditional medical approach, not a substitute for it. The reason this was so important was that the real choice we would be offering ourselves, as well as the children, would be one between conflict and peace. If as an organization we were to make the mistake of confronting the medical establishment, we would be practicing the opposite of what we had set out to accomplish. The advice I still give to any parent who brings their child to me is, "Listen to everything your doctor tells you, but do not internalize what *anyone* tells you about the limits to your future chances, because at this Center we know that your chances for freedom, happiness, and peace are without any limit at all."

We Can Begin Only Now

Those of us who joined together to start the Center shared the conviction that our real satisfaction and inner healing would come through our service to others. The wish to be of genuine help requires no long-range plans or dreams of expansion. We have worked hard to remain free of that kind of future orientation. Our interest was in broadening our perceptions and not in changing sick bodies into well bodies. Our central focus was to take an entirely new look at our own concepts of life and death and thereby to free our thoughts of fear.

I have noticed that a great deal of strife can result if people come together to pursue a purely external goal, even if the goal is very idealistic. They will attack each other whenever they perceive that another member of the group is standing in the way of the task that has been agreed upon. This they do in the name of a greater good. For example, they will think that another group member's feelings are not as important as the sick children they are all there to help. What is not realized is that only people with healed relationships are in a position to give the kind of help that will last. It is peace we want to extend, and to extend peace we must first have it.

In 1975, a small group of us—Gloria Murray, Patsy Robinson, Pat Taylor, and myself—met and formed The Center for Attitudinal Healing.* From the very beginning there has never been a charge for any service we have offered. We began with a few young children who had catastrophic illnesses such as cancer and muscular dystrophy or life-threatening conditions resulting from traumatic accidents. We soon discovered that the siblings and parents of the children needed support from each other, and so groups for them were also formed. Later we added groups for adults and young adults and for children whose parents have cancer. When AIDS first began to affect so many people in the Bay area, we added groups for everyone touched by this epidemic.

---

*The Center for Attitudinal Healing is presently located at 33 Buchanan Street, Sausalito, California 94965.

In the traditional model, the physician attempts to do something to the patient. Our goal at the Center is to be an educational model for self-learning. We administer no treatment. Since we are interested not in healing bodies but in healing minds, we define *healing* as the letting go of fear and *health* as inner peace. We join with those who come into the Center with the mutual goal of freeing our minds of fear—fear of ourselves, of relationships, of illness, and of death.

It is quite possible that the fear of death is behind every other terror we hold. I am certain this fear was part of my reason for starting the Center. Since children had always been my greatest teachers, I must have sensed that they would also be the ones from whom I would learn that even this ultimate fear is groundless. And indeed they teach this to all of us in a most beautiful way. When adults see these inwardly peaceful and joyous children on television, or standing before an auditorium full of people, or in person at our Center, their fear of death subsides, at least a little. I believe it is because before them is living proof that we can be happy and live lives that deeply benefit other people at the very time we have one of the world's most dreaded illnesses or conditions. These children have taught me that our capacity to be happy and useful cannot truly be hampered by external conditions, even bodily ones, and that death will not frighten us if we decide to give to others from our internal treasure of love and peace.

Although my guidance was to have a place where some of the principles of *A Course in Miracles* could be demonstrated, it was also my guidance that the *Course* itself should not be taught or even recommended at the Center. Please do not confuse Attitudinal Healing with *A Course in Miracles*, for they are not the same. Most of the people involved at our Center are not students of the *Course*, but they are in general agreement with the principles of Attitudinal Healing, which are largely based on the *Course*. Although these principles have a universal spiritual base, the Center is not a religious organization, and the parents' or children's backgrounds or beliefs are of no concern to us. Anyone with a physical or emotional condition that one of our groups or projects deals with is wholly welcomed.

The principles of Attitudinal Healing have been expanded since *Teach Only Love* was first published in 1983. There are now twelve principles, which are used in Centers throughout the world. It was my original guidance to use some selected lessons from the *Course* to serve as a basis for learning how to change our attitudes. I chose lessons from the Workbook of *A Course in Miracles* that did not mention the word *God*, or have any religious terminology. I did not want our principles to frighten away those who did not believe in God or did not want to be involved in anything that seemed religious.

I believe our twelve principles have a universal appeal that crosses cultural and religious barriers. I have repeatedly seen how peoples' lives are transformed when these principles have become their heartbeat, their way of looking at themselves, and their way of communicating with others. Perhaps the best way to tell you about the principles is to talk about the Center and the children who have put them into practice. I will be doing that for the remainder of this book through the use of examples, many of which will be the stories of children with catastrophic illnesses. I have found these young people to be very powerful and inspirational teachers. If children with life-threatening diseases can attain inner peace, need we whose problems appear to be much less severe settle for a lesser goal?

Here, then, are the twelve principles of Attitudinal Healing:

1. *The essence of our being is love.* Love cannot be hindered by what is merely physical. Therefore, we believe the mind has no limits; nothing is impossible; and all disease is potentially reversible. And because love is eternal, death need not be viewed fearfully.

2. *Health is inner peace.* Healing is letting go of fear. To make changing the body our goal is to fail to recognize that our single goal is peace of mind.

3. *Giving and receiving are the same.* When our attention is on giving and joining with others, fear is removed and we accept healing for ourselves.

4. *We can let go of the past and the future.* We experience inner peace when we let go of our attachments to the painful past and the fearful future and learn to live in the present.

5. *Now is the only time there is.* Pain, grief, depression, guilt, and other forms of fear disappear when the mind is focused in loving peace on this instant.

6. *We learn to love ourselves and others by forgiving rather than judging.* Forgiveness is the way to true health and happiness. When we choose to see everyone as a teacher of forgiveness, each moment gives us an opportunity for happiness, peace, and love.

7. *We can become love-finders rather than faultfinders.* Regardless of what another person's behavior might

be, we can always choose to see only the light of love in that person.

8. *We can be peaceful inside regardless of what is happening outside*. Despite the chaos in our lives, we can choose to be peaceful, knowing that we are connected and sustained by our loving, peaceful Source.

9. *We are students and teachers to each other*. Peace comes to us when we recognize and demonstrate that all our relationships are equal.

10. *We can focus on the whole of our lives rather than on the fragments*. It is an illusion to believe that our lives are separate from each other. Healing is focusing on our interconnectedness with each other and all living things.

11. *Because love is eternal, death need not be viewed as fearful*. We begin to let go of our fear of death when we truly believe that what is real never changes and that Love is always present.

12. *We can always see ourselves and others as extending love or giving a call for help*. Rather than seeing anger and attack, it is always possible for us to recognize a call for help and to answer with love.

Kaycee Poirier from Shawnigan Lake, British Columbia, wrote me that she felt our principles might be a little too complex for children to understand. She then rewrote the principles for us, and several months before she died, the Center began to use her adaptations, a loving gift from a wonderful eleven-year-old girl.

Children's Version of Principles of Attitudinal Healing

1. Love is one of the most important things in life!

2. It is important to get better—so we must not let fear trap us!

3. Giving and receiving are the same thing.

4. Don't live in the past and don't live in the future.

5. Do what you can now. Each minute is for giving love.

6. We can learn to love ourselves and others by forgiving instead of not forgiving. Example: fighting.

7. We can find love instead of fault.

8. If something is the matter outside, don't go crazy because you are safe inside.

9. We are students and teachers to each other.

10. Don't just look at the bad things, look at the good things too!

11. Since love is eternal, death need not be scary.

12. We can always see other people as giving love or asking for help.

Seven
We Are Love

The principles of Attitudinal Healing are interdependent and interrelated, especially the first one, which is the key to Attitudinal Healing and unites and flows through all of the others. As I continue to discuss them and give examples, you will see how they overlap and that each discussion and example generally includes aspects of other principles. The first principle of Attitudinal Healing is

The essence of our being is love. Love cannot be hindered by what is merely physical. Therefore, we believe the mind has no limits; nothing is impossible; and all disease is potentially reversible. And because love is eternal, death need not be viewed fearfully.

This principle is based on the premise that our true identity is spiritual rather than physical. Love is the part of us that is real. Because love itself is our potential, we are not limited by the body and are not subject to any of the body's conditions or "laws." Love is everything there is and the only thing that is real.

Communication with others is from love to love and not from our past experiences to theirs. No two past experiences are identical, and communication that rests on judgments is inherently conflicted. Yet when communication is based on love, it is deeply satisfying and healing. Even our fear that death could interrupt it begins to vanish.

What, then, is love? Because it must be experienced in order to be meaningful, I can't define it for you except to say that it is the total absence of fear and the recognition of complete union with all life. We love another when we see that our interests are not separate. This is always a union of higher minds and not an alliance of egos.

It isn't possible to evaluate or prove love in the usual ways. The fact that we are not able to measure it does not make it less real. We have all had glimpses of pure, unconditional love, and there is unquestionably a part of us that knows it exists. We become aware of love whenever we choose to accept people without judging them and commence the gentle effort of giving without any thought of getting something in return. This means, for example, that true love is not giving in order to change another's attitude from a bad mood to one of light-heartedness or from ingratitude to one of thanks to us. True love is a completely pure and unencumbered form of giving. It is extended freely to the love in others and is its own reward.

The word *love*, as we generally use it, means something quite different from real love. It is conditional love—giving in order to get. It is a bargain, a trade arrangement. This is often fairly obvious in romantic relationships in which each partner is giving with the expectation that it will be returned in the specific form that is desired. Conditional love is also what passes for kindness in most parent/child relationships. Here, the extension of love is contingent on approved behavior and attitudes. Parents frequently seek an affirmation of their own worth through the accomplishments of their child and through "payments" of respect. Children often love their parents only when they get what they think they want, whether this be a new possession or approval and praise. Such love is neither dependable nor permanent, and its temporary nature causes us to carry the underlying fear that we are about to be abandoned.

When we are giving true love, our concern is not with our own or anyone else's behavior. We feel natural because we recognize that love is our natural state. We are not aware of limitations. We don't question the possibility of devotion, and we are not preoccupied with time. We are only conscious of now and all it contains. When we are extending love, we are free and at peace. Attitudinal Healing shows us how to allow ourselves to experience this kind of love—the only love that is eternal.

Love Is Our Essence

We all say that we want to have less conflict, fear, stress, and depression. And deep within our hearts we do want this. But on the level from which we function most of the time, we rarely choose peace over conflict and happiness over fear because of the sacrifices we believe this choice must entail. We also believe that there is satisfaction in revenge, that we can be right by proving someone else wrong, that to humble someone who is being difficult will give us "a little peace and quiet." It seems logical to us to be stern with our children in order to teach them gentleness. We think that there are people who deserve to lose because of their behavior and that the pain they receive is just. We try to increase love with one person by excluding others. We mistake guilt for attraction; we believe that pain can be pleasurable and that taking is getting. Then we are puzzled as to why this approach to life does not bring us peace, and yet we see no reason to change our basic beliefs.

It is obvious that we need an experience which will bring clarity to our mind. The experience we all need more of is love. In order to move more deeply into an atmosphere of love, we must identify less with the body and more with our love-related emotions. These are the feelings that speak to us of what has always been within us but what our shabby self-image has not allowed us to see. To recognize it we have to bring it forth, for only by extending what is good can we know and believe in the good within us and that we ourselves are good. However, to bring it out does not always mean to act it out but rather to bring it into our hearts and minds.

A preoccupation with the body and its behavior does not allow love to flood our mood, because the body is merely what is different and separate. In order to love, we must recognize what is the same within us and all living things. The love in us can unite with the love in others, but two bodies can never become one.

Emotions that center on the body and exclude others are negative or self-denying. As a first step, we must honestly and gently question our investment in how our body looks—in how we have adorned it, honored it, and employed it and in how we calculate the fair amount of credit, thanks, influence, money, or popularity that our body should receive. To the degree that we value our body identity, we tend to downplay or ignore altogether our real identity, which is love.

This gentle questioning does not call for impulsive or drastic changes in behavior or lifestyle. It calls for nothing more than simple, calm noticing, especially inner noticing. Once we recognize our true value, if any external changes are needed, these will occur naturally and in their own time. If we become preoccupied with what we do rather than how we do it, we needlessly delay ourselves. Attitudinal Healing is concerned only with how. Are we acting with love, with peace, with happiness, and with certainty? If we are, whatever we do will promote those states.

A preoccupation with other people's bodies and bodily behavior leads us to believe that our body determines what kind of person we are and what kind of relationships we must settle for. We may get momentary pleasure from the fact that others seem less attractive than we do, and some people may be drawn to us because of our personality or special accomplishments, but we always know in our heart that relationships based on such things are shallow and fleeting. We really don't want people to be attracted to us because of our bodies but because of what there is about us that is changeless and timeless. We want people to understand us and love us because they truly see us. They cannot do this while relating to us only as a body. We want to be aware, and we want others to be aware, of the golden glow from within and not merely the glitter of surface appearances. The part of us with which we identify determines this outcome. What we put forth, mentally and emotionally, is what others relate to. We are either extending gentleness, joy, kindness, openness, and peace or we are hiding behind a purely physical identification. We can't do both, because one is love and the other is fear.

Nothing Real Is Impossible

This concept was life-changing for Colleen Mulvihill, a twenty-three-year-old woman who was a senior working toward a Movement Education degree at a liberal-arts college in Northern California. Colleen was pretty enough to model, and she sometimes did. When I first met her, she also had two year-round, part-time jobs, one as a sports-medicine coordinator in her college athletic department and the other as a tutor in the school's developmental-movement laboratory where children with neurological and academic handicaps are helped to develop motor skills. During the summer months, she had assumed the additional job of teaching swimming and crafts at a nearby day camp. Colleen lived in a small apartment five hundred miles away from her family, and her best friend was a German shepherd named Sasha, a seeing-eye dog.

When she came to me, Colleen was legally blind. (This term applies to those whose sight is so limited that they cannot function as sighted, although they may have a small amount of close vision.) From birth, she has had a condition known as retrolental fibroplasia, which is a progressive accumulation of scar tissue behind the retina that may eventually cause blindness or at least severely limited vision.

When she was born, it was standard medical practice to put premature infants into high-pressure oxygen tanks. Later in life she was told that it was this procedure that had caused her blindness. Possibly you can imagine the rage and resentment a person with this condition might have against the world. Indeed, Colleen had such feelings as well as a great deal of pain that is often associated with this type of disease.

She was born and raised in the Los Angeles area by parents who saw value in her attending regular public school rather than special schools for the handicapped. They reasoned that this would better prepare her for the real world. It was obviously a good decision for Colleen, although there is, of course, no right or wrong procedure that can be applied to all cases involving handicapped children. With the understanding assistance of teachers who always seated her in the front of the room and gave her additional auditory and visual cues, she graduated from both elementary and high school and then decided on a small college away from home.

This intelligent and highly spirited girl found her situation more difficult as her limited vision continued to diminish. Sasha, a two-year-old seeing-eye dog, came into Colleen's life. She and Sasha trained together in North Hollywood and have been inseparable companions ever since. Sasha accompanied her to college classes and even to the state Capitol in Sacramento, where Colleen was an active lobbyist for the National Federation of the Blind.

Several years ago, Colleen became aware that many people were discussing supplements to traditional medical procedures, and she began to hear evidence that the mind can affect the body. It was shortly after this that she began to visit me. I introduced her to *A Course in Miracles*.

Later, I referred her to the adult Attitudinal Healing group at our Center. I emphasized to her that the mind has no boundaries and that nothing is impossible. I told her to let go of every negative value she ever had and not to limit herself to her past beliefs or confine herself to a reality that came to her only through her physical senses.

We talked about this very important concept from *A Course in Miracles*:

There is no order of difficulty in miracles.*

Miracles can be defined as shifts in perception that remove the blocks to our awareness of love's presence. Therefore, they can be seen as a natural occurrence. Although miracles are not physical phenomena, changes at the physical level may sometimes accompany them. I shared with Colleen my conviction that we can learn to shift our perception and see the presence of love, and that this is true sight.

One day, Colleen asked a question that was very important to her. "Is it possible for me to regain my sight?" I replied, "Anything is possible. You do not have to be a negative statistic on a probability curve of people with rentrolental fibroplasia."

She began to grasp the idea that the thoughts we put into our minds determine our perceptions. She began to work on "positive mental pictures" and to practice the principles in *A Course in Miracles*. Practicing peace of mind and the peace of God became her single goal; practicing forgiveness became her single function; and listening to, and being directed by, her inner voice became her way of experiencing a sense of completion and oneness. She began to forgive God and the universe for her blindness. Her bitterness dissolved and was replaced by an increasing sense of peace. As this happened, her head and neck pains began to ease.

Gradually, a subtle but quite genuine change began to take place in the way Colleen saw herself. She told me later, "It was as though my attitude about myself began to shift. Where I had always treated myself as a blind person, I now began to think of myself as normal." Even so, Colleen was totally unprepared when her daytime vision suddenly began to improve enough so that she could see where she was going. Her ophthalmologist informed her that she was now legally sighted during the daytime, although she remained legally blind at night. When I talked to him on the phone, he stated that he had never seen a person with Colleen's condition make this kind of visual improvement.

Her increasing ability to see brought a new set of problems involving Sasha. "It is very traumatic," Colleen explained, "for a guide dog to find she is not essential for the totality of her master's mobility." But that problem, too, was gradually solved as she and Sasha worked together for a new understanding of each other's needs.

Colleen continued in school to prepare herself to be of service to others who are ill. She is primarily interested in the holistic health approach in which one attempts to assist the whole person rather than to treat only sick organs. She has helped many people at our Center and in other cities and has been active in our telephone network, working with blind people on the phone throughout the United States.

Recently, Colleen called me. "Jerry," she said, "I want to take you for a drive."

"What do you mean?" I asked.

"I am now licensed to drive a car in two different states and am legally sighted for both day and night." I want you to know that my drive with Colleen Mulvihill was the happiest time I have ever had in a car, even though I cried.

There are many times I forget some of the principles mentioned in this book, and I end up depressed. When I see Colleen and experience her unconditional love, I am aware that she also sees the light in me. This helps me to let go of feelings of darkness by reminding me of my true reality. To me, Colleen brings to life Jesus' statement: "I have come into the world to give sight to those who are spiritually blind and to show those who think that they see that they are blind." *Judgment is blind. Only love sees.*

Love Is Eternal

It is clear that we will never know peace as long as we think of ourselves as vulnerable to sickness and accident, growing old, becoming feeble, and dying. Without a change in perception about what we are, anxiety will continue to underlie all we think and do as we anticipate the approach of our final annihilation. Somehow we must begin to recognize that we live now and eternally as love. I believe we are in this world only to learn and teach love. The lengths of our assignments vary, but what each of us gives and is given is the same: love.

Working with children who are facing death, and also with their families, has helped me overcome my own fear of death and to question the belief that death is final. You might wonder how we at the Center can work intimately with these youngsters, watch some of them die, and yet not destroy ourselves emotionally. Speaking for myself, I could not continue if I still held to the belief that death is the end of life. If I really thought that, these children's deaths would indeed tear me up too much to go on.

Most of us at the Center try to look at death as a transition. We feel blessed to know these youngsters and their families. They teach us that there is a difference between life and the body, that the body is temporary but life, being spirit, is unending. Their message has been one of life—eternal life—and the powerful lesson that living is synonymous with loving.

The first of the Center's children to die was Greg Harrison. He was eleven years old. When there were no more new drugs to be administered and it appeared he didn't have much time left, Greg was asked by the other children in his group, "What do you think it will be like to die?" I will never forget his answer: "I think that when you die, you just discard your body, which was never real in the first place. Then you are in Heaven, at one with all souls. And sometimes you come back to earth and act as a guardian angel to somebody. I think that's what I would like to do." Greg's attitude toward death shows that any occurrence in this world can be looked at with love. And it is, of course, such a relief to do so.

Another member of our Center family, Will Stein, a fourteen-year-old with Ewing's sarcoma, taped an interview with me two weeks before he died. It was his belief that we all agree to certain assignments before being born into this world. Some are for long periods, others are shorter, but the length of time doesn't matter. Will felt his assignment was a short one but that while he was still breathing, his assignment was not over.

As long as our bodies are alive, our job is to use them as a means of extending love in a form that others can recognize and receive. Because of the basic gentleness of their spirits, many children demonstrate how love can be extended even when they are not in a physical position to do good deeds. It is what we do with out hearts that affects others most deeply. It is not the movements of our body or the words within our mind that transmit love. We love from heart to heart.

There is, of course, no rule as to how a loved one is to be remembered. And an appearance of peace and joy should never be forced. However, during the course of a child's illness, some parents come to the realization that their child is more than a body, and they then know that their relationship with this beloved child will not end with death. I am convinced this is not deception but the recognition of reality. When death occurs, it makes what these parents feel after their child has gone not only bearable but peaceful, because they continue to feel joined with their child through love.

The attitude of Bryan Bradshaw's family following his death is an illustration of an emphasis on spiritual reality rather than on bodies. Bryan was an eight-year-old who had one leg amputated as a result of bone cancer. His courage was remarkable, and he and his family were strong teachers to us all.

About a week before Bryan died, I visited the family in San Jose and spent some time with his six-year-old sister, Lorrie Ann. I asked her to draw a picture about what was going on in her mind. It showed Bryan with wings on his sides going up to Heaven. She said, "When you are in Heaven, there is no sickness or pain. You are just happy and feel love because you talk to God all the time."

One of our staff members and I went to San Jose to be with Bryan's family the day he died. We were impressed by their sense of peace. We saw that many tearful friends who came to their home were helped by their calming influence. Some of the children who were there felt guilty because they had not visited Bryan as much as they thought they should have. They, along with Bryan's parents, went with us to the family room to talk things out. After a while, the children's guilt lessened, and they began telling funny stories of the good times they had had with Bryan. Whenever we lose interest in guilt, only love remains.

Since Bryan's family had no religious preference, they asked Tom Pinkson, a friend of the Center, and me to conduct a memorial service that would allow those attending to leave feeling happier than when they came. I began my remarks by sharing Lorrie Ann's picture and her comments about it. Tom talked about the many ways in which Bryan and his family had helped others. And we both told about the feelings we had experienced in Bryan's presence and the beauty and love we were feeling that day. Then the entire group joined in singing some of Bryan's favorite songs. We were led by Rabbi Nathan Segal, who had become friends with Bryan at a Center picnic.

Following the service, helium balloons were given to everyone. Bryan loved balloons. At the same moment, we released a hundred of them along with our individual mes-

sages of love to Bryan and the universe. The balloons appeared
to join together in a rainbow and float into the sky. Several
parents came up and said how much they had dreaded bringing their children to the memorial service and how surprised
and relieved they were to experience happiness rather than
grief on such an occasion.

We Need Fear Nothing

Those, of course, are not the only children from our Center
who have died. I have mentioned these few because each of
them has personally taught me a lesson strongly related to the
words *Death need not be viewed fearfully*. A fearful perception is
of no use to anyone. And my work at the Center has shown me
how genuinely helpful it is to look at all things in peace. It is
only a gentle vision that allows us to see that what we are—and
all that we are—is pure love.

I remember an all-day meeting we had at the Center for
about twenty-five families who had each lost a child. Many of
these children had not attended our groups, but the comments
and stories related by their parents reminded me of the inner
core that unites every person on this earth. We are all members of a single family and each person is our brother and sister, even though we often forget this.

A number of the parents at this meeting said that even
while dying their child had been their teacher and that in
many respects the traditional roles of parent and child had
been reversed. And all of the parents stated that the loving
spirit of their child seemed to continue as a strong and comforting presence in their heart and that in many ways they felt
a continuation of the actual relationship. This, they said, was a
deeply healing experience.

Many things we do not understand simply because we are not yet in a position to do so. This is why patience with other people's experiences and points of view is not only a comfort to them but a relief to us as well. Love overlooks differences, for it notices something of far greater importance: how much alike we are because how much like love itself we are. Once we see this honestly, we quickly begin to lose our fear of others and to gain confidence in our potential harmlessness as well. The more we enfold others in this harmlessness, through releasing our own mind of defensiveness and suspicion, the more we begin to glimpse the vast harmlessness of the universe and how utterly impossible it would be for any living thing to suffer for very long in any true sense. There is an end to pain. There is a point beyond which misery cannot go. Never are we left comfortless.

Eight
Our Goal Is Peace

To know peace we must recognize what there is within us that is already at peace. The place of peace is found within our mind. The body cannot tell us how to feel because the source of our experience is our mind, regardless of how we choose to use it. We are not a victim of the body and our mind cannot truly be threatened. For this reason there is always a way to freedom. That is why the second principle of Attitudinal Healing is

> *Health is inner peace. Healing is letting go of fear.* To make changing the body our goal is to fail to recognize that our single goal is peace of mind.

In Attitudinal Healing, when we talk about health we do not focus on the body but on the heart and the contents of our mind. Regardless of the state of our body, we know that our natural state of mind is peace and love. Anyone who chooses to can have inner peace. Healing is letting go of fear, because when our mind releases fear it returns to its natural state of love and peace and naturally extends them into every aspect of our life.

What Is Our Real Identity?

To have inner rest and contentment and an increasing experience of freedom and release, it is necessary for us to question our old sense of identity. Are we really only a body that lives a little while and then dies? Does the body set the limits to our strength, dictate how we must feel, and define the tiny range of activities in which we can engage? Or is there a potential within us that knows no limit of any kind and is unending in its capacity to make us happy and set us free?

There is no point beyond which the combined power of the mind and will cannot go, because when united they allow thought to be flooded with love. Today there are many thought systems which acknowledge that the body is not a limit on the mind, that there is a reality beyond what physical eyes see and ears hear that awaits our recognition, and that a single Source unites all minds on a level that we can experience here and now.

There often appears to be a philosophical and spiritual joining of East and West within these teachings. Most of these systems teach that the thoughts we hold determine our experience and then explain how we can change our perceptions of ourselves and the world. Attitudinal Healing has a similar objective, because once we begin to remove the barriers to our perception of love's presence, we have begun to heal ourselves on every level and in every way.

There are countless examples of people who, after serious illness or accidents, astound their doctors by their will to live and undergo remarkable rehabilitations. Others, in spite of severe disabilities, lead happy, loving lives. This does not mean that our goal is physical healing or that if we do not heal our bodies we are somehow wrong. Our goal is peace now—this very instant. Thus it is central to our happiness that our years, whether long or short, be free of fear and anger and that our body be used as a means for giving others the gift of kindness.

Each of us, to experience peace, must recognize that we have a choice as to whether we view our identity as severely limited and small or as unlimited and full of love. We do not have to set any boundaries on our health or happiness because our doctor, parents, friends, the media, or society may have told us that there will always be things we cannot change. The attitudinal healer does not counsel anyone to adjust to pain and death or to compromise with misery, because it is possible for all of us to quietly listen to our inner guide, who will lead us to freedom. Love knows no place it cannot go and no mind it cannot bring to rest.

Within Good There Is No Limit

We spend a great deal of time at the Center reminding each other that nothing is impossible. Tinman Walker has been, and continues to be, a very effective teacher of this concept. When he was fourteen he collided with a truck while riding his bike down a hill. Due to the severity of his injuries, there was little hope for his survival. After a subdural hematoma (a mass of blood under the covering of the brain) was removed, he remained in a coma. The medical team caring for him held little hope for his regaining consciousness, and if he did, they said he would be a vegetable. When he was sent home, still comatose, the family was advised to put him in an institution. However, believing in the healing power of love, they had other ideas for his care.

Eighty-one days after his accident, Tinman awakened. He had a spastic paralysis on the right side of his body and his speech was labored and difficult to understand. He was given the best physical and occupational therapy his parents could find, and in time, he was able to return to school.

Prior to his accident, Tinman had been an outstanding athlete, but now he was barely able to walk. Because of his physical handicaps, he saw himself as a social outcast. Much of his time was spent at home, friendless and alone.

After three and a half years, a speech therapist who was evaluating him said that Tinman had made about all the progress he was going to make. At that point, he and his family became discouraged and decided to seek help from our Center, because they had heard that we believe nothing is impossible.

When Tinman first came to us, he was severely limited in many ways. His speech was slow and halting, and because of the degree of paralysis that still remained, he walked very deliberately and with a limp. But what impressed me most about him when we first met was the sparkle in his eyes. Immediately, I had a strong feeling he and I were going to be significant teachers to each other and that miracles were to be expected.

A week after we met, I was given two theater tickets and asked him to join me. He agreed. But first we went to a restaurant, where he had considerable difficulty eating. It not only took him a long time to finish dinner, but after we left, he had difficulty walking up the San Francisco streets. I could see what a great teacher of patience he was going to be to me and must already have been to his family.

Tinman spent a lot of time with the group at the Center and much one-to-one time with me. He also found a physical therapist who was willing to work with him. We all had one goal. We were determined to see that Tinman turn out to be much more than a negative statistic. And when two or more minds join to achieve a single loving goal—watch out!

We began to make open-loop tapes that he could play during his sleep. At first, only my voice was on them, but later he used his own. "Open-loop" tapes are cassette tapes designed to repeat continuously a three- to five-minute recording. They are simple to use, widely available, and very effective.

On the initial tape, I suggested to Tinman that he view his brain as a blackboard and erase from it any memory of a time he had difficulty with his speech. In place of these scenes of distress, I instructed him to picture scenes in which a steady improvement in his speech pattern occurred. Similar suggestions were made regarding his walking difficulties, his spastic paralysis, and other related problems. In this way, every night negative pictures were being erased mentally and replaced by positive pictures of his functioning more freely. These mental pictures were to be visualized in specific form, such as seeing himself skiing and driving a car.

About a month later, Tinman came to my office and asked me to watch him. He said he was going to put a hole right where he was standing. With glee, he jumped about six inches off the floor and landed—still standing. It was the first time he could do this since his accident.

The other young people in Tinman's group at the Center were very patient with him. He liked to tell jokes, and to most of us it seemed that he took forever to finish a story. Later, he told me that the Center had been the first place where people were patient enough to listen to his stories without interrupting or trying to finish his sentences for him. As we go through the day, we often become anxious to save time. But is there really a better use of our time than to listen to another in love?

After Tinman's speech had improved, he found another use for positive mental imagery. At one meeting, he told us he was having a tough time with Italian classes at school. Every time he took an oral exam, he froze up and was unable to give the correct answer. I suggested that he close his eyes and think of himself in a place where he felt completely relaxed. For Tinman, this was in the mountains. I then had him erase all the old tapes in his mind of when he had done poorly on examinations and replace them with positive tapes showing himself as calm, relaxed, and answering test questions correctly. I also suggested that he view his teacher as a friend trying to help him rather than as an enemy seeking to find his weaknesses and embarrass him. I suggested that he practice this imagery each morning upon awakening and just before he went to sleep at night until the next test. If he became fearful while doing his imagery, he was to pause and visualize himself as relaxed in the mountains. He was then to proceed with this "positive active imagination" until he could do it five times in a row without experiencing fear.

At the next meeting, Tinman excitedly told us of his great success on the Italian test. Other kids in the group admitted they were also having trouble with tests, so he became a teacher to them, again proving the far-reaching influence of a positive belief system.

Perhaps the high point in my work with Tinman was an event that drew tears of happiness to my eyes. I was going to give a lecture to a group of physicians in Los Angeles and asked him to join me. He replied, with a smile on his face, that he wouldn't be able to because he was going cross-country skiing.

We Are More Than a Body

Joe Marks is another example of a child going beyond the seeming limitations of his body—beyond what was thought even remotely possible. I'm going to let his mother, Mary Marks, tell you part of Joe's story.

Working one night in Southern California, where I was studying at a chiropractic college, I received a phone call informing me that my two boys, who were living with their father and stepmother in Northern California, had been in an accident with a tractor. The younger one was unhurt, but they thought I should get up there because they didn't know if the older boy was going to pull through.

No planes were flying directly from Los Angeles to Eureka, so it took me fifteen hours to arrive at the hospital. I found my twelve-and-a-half-year-old lying in the critical care unit naked under a sheet with a huge bandage on his head, his leg in traction, several intravenous bottles dripping into him, and various tubes, including two in his nose—one for oxygen and the other pumping his stomach. It was an incredible sight and not the boy I had seen a few weeks before, who was a normal, healthy preteenager. The accident had left him with broken ribs, three fractures of the pelvis, his right thigh broken in half, multiple skull fractures—the whole base of his skull was in little pieces—and spinal fluid leaking from his ear. His head looked like a crushed watermelon. He was not expected to live very long.

Without going into any more gory details, I can say that so many of his functions were impaired he couldn't breathe, and among other complications, he had developed pneumonia. The EEG brain-wave tests showed nothing but slow rolling waves—almost flat—indicating that if Joe, by some miracle, did live, he would be a vegetable, unable to move or think. As for the rest of him, there wasn't much to do for broken ribs, and at first, they just had his leg in traction without setting it; later, they used pins and a cast so that he could be moved more easily.

We stayed with Joe twenty-four hours a day. There wasn't much else we could do for him. Yet recently, when someone suggested that I visualize a beautiful place, my thoughts went to that intensive-care ward and sitting next to Joe. There was nothing left of that boy but pure love. He seemed blank, not to be participating at all. His eyes never moved, and even when his fingers were pinched, his nervous system was so depressed there wasn't even a primitive response. And he lay there like that for three months; yet for me it was a joy just to be there with him. It seemed like the whole state of California knew that Joe had been hurt. There were constant prayers for him and a regular meditation at nine o'clock every evening. The whole room seemed to light up, and Joe would seem to glow just lying there without giving any response. People would come in just to be with him and often commented on a kind of love or energy they felt being there. That of course, reinforced my own ability to express love to him.

After about five weeks it was recommended that he be institutionalized, but we didn't accept that. So we made arrangements to take him to a hospital on an Indian reservation near where his father and his family lived. It was a very small place with just nine beds supervised by a physician who had been a good friend of the family.

Suddenly, I found I had a lot of input into Joe's life. The doctor was very interested in nutrition and asked me to govern Joe's diet. He had been getting a sort of milk shake through the tube in his nose. I changed the formula to include a lot of ground-up vitamins and minerals; I made him a bunch of brightly colored gowns to replace the white ones he wore; I washed him, brushed his teeth for him, and combed the little bit of hair that was growing back. We played rock music and classical music in his room all the time, and sitting there in that room became my home, my whole existence.

I spent a lot of time holding and stroking Joe. Then we'd move his arms and legs and turn him to avoid bedsores. He was supposed to have the bed cranked up for better circulation, but instead I would hold him upright and hug him a lot. Of course, he was completely out of it, but he was my kid; I loved him and it didn't matter that the only response I got was the warmth of his body.

Then even that little hospital began saying there was no justification for his being there any longer. He had improved in many ways. The pneumonia was gone, as was the kidney infection and catheter. The tracheotomy tube had been removed; the scars were healing; the bones mending. He was ticking away, but not awake. He was in a coma, and they wanted us to take him somewhere else.

Just before the Marks family had to take Joe out of the hospital, he began to respond: first by squeezing his father's hand; later, by moving a leg upon his mother's request. Not only could he hear her voice, despite the fact that his eardrums had been punctured and all the bones shattered, but he was following commands.

When Mary Marks heard about her son's accident that first September night, her immediate reaction had been anger. The feeling lasted only a few moments before her attitudes and feelings began to shift.

I started a mental dialogue with Joe, telling him that I understood, that everything was OK, that if his spirit needed to leave, it was all right. Either way, I told him

mentally, he would be fine. I didn't really pray for his heal-
ing as much as I constantly prayed for understanding of
what had happened.

It is most difficult to convey to you the devotion, acceptance, and love that his father, Keith; his stepmother, Sharon;
and his mother, Mary, showered on Joe. They all felt that Joe
was a part of the family, no matter what shape he was in, and
they fully intended that he should experience this sense of
belonging at all times.

It was after the end of his stay at the reservation hospital
in Hoopa that Joe's grandmother mentioned my name to
Mary. She was a student of *A Course in Miracles* and had heard
me lecture about the mind being limitless. She had also been
impressed with the story of Tinman Walker. Joe's doctor
phoned and asked me to consult on the case. I flew to Eureka,
where he was going to meet me and fly us to the small town of
Hoopa. However, a storm prevented any further air travel, so
we ended up driving.

We finally found the trailer where Joe and his mother were
living. Joe was lying in bed looking extremely sad. He was not
able to talk and was completely blind with bilateral optic atro-
phy. He was almost completely paralyzed. In spite of all of this,
I felt a spirit of positive expectation, a "We can" attitude coming from Joe, his mother, and even the very atmosphere within
that tiny trailer.

I explained to Joe and his mother about our work at the
Center, and I related the story of Tinman and other youngsters
we have seen. I emphasized our belief that minds are joined and
that nothing is impossible, and I told them about a project of
ours headed by Tammy Cohen and, later, Cheryl Balsan, in
which we were teaching blind children to sense colors and

objects without touching them. I mentioned to Joe that there was a fourteen-year-old blind boy named Harold Alexander who could not only identify colors but also ride his bicycle and do many other things that most people wouldn't have expected— or believed. Joe became intrigued with these possibilities.

For the next hour, we experienced together some aspects of the fact that minds are joined. I would send Joe the thoughts "red" or "blue." He would nod his head vertically for red, horizontally for blue. Within the hour, he was 80 percent accurate in identifying the right colors, and his depression began to disappear. He even became quite animated.

I told Joe that his mind was not limited to his body, and I shared with him this lesson from the *Course*:

I am not a body. I am free. For I am still as God created me.*

I also suggested three other things to him. First, that he could imagine movies in his mind in which he saw himself walking and talking. Second, that since he still had faith in God, he could join with God, erase all doubts, and accept the fact that in a few days he was going to fly to Los Angeles to enter a special rehabilitation hospital for the neurologically damaged. I suggested that although he might not believe that anyone in the world could be worse off than he was, when he got to the hospital it would be beneficial for him to find someone else he could help.

About a month later, I received a letter from Mary. She told me that Joe had been experiencing periods of deep sadness. On his ward, there was a small child who was suffering from an irritation to the central nervous system and was crying all the time. No drug seemed to help. Mary remembered what I had said about Joe's helping someone, and all of a sudden she found herself picking up this small child and carrying him over to Joe's bed. She plopped him onto his lap.

At first, Joe looked startled. Then, with his left hand, which had a little movement in it, he began to gently stroke the child, who stopped crying almost immediately. Mary described the situation as if both children had risen to a higher state of consciousness, where there was only bliss and peace.

I flew to Southern California several times to visit Joe and his family. On one visit, I took Tinman Walker with me. The timing was perfect. Joe, his stepmother, and his mother were getting discouraged. Tinman walked in and began telling Joe that he was doing things the doctors never thought possible and that Joe could do them also. "You just have to keep saying, 'I can; nothing is impossible,' and keep getting rid of all your doubts." Later, Joe's family said that seeing Tinman was worth more than what anyone else had said to them or anything they had read. It was the first time they had actually met someone who had been in a state similar to Joe's who had truly made it. A couple of months later, with some assistance, Joe began to walk.

Later I went to Fullerton, California, with members of our staff and some of our children to make a presentation at a conference. I phoned Mary the night before to see how things were going. She was exuberant. Joe had started talking! I asked if they would be interested in coming to the conference and participating; her response was an ecstatic "Yes!"

On the day of the conference, the auditorium was filled with health professionals. When it was Joe's turn to speak, he got up and said, "You never know for sure what another person can do in the future. Look at me. I was supposed to be a vegetable. Tell your patients never to give up, that nothing is impossible—just look at me." Tears came to my eyes and I think to everyone else's as well.

On another occasion I took Harold Alexander, who was blind, and his girlfriend to see Joe. That weekend was an experience I will never forget. Can you imagine how I felt after we got on the plane and discovered that Harold had never flown before? To be able to share a blind person's first experience on an airplane was a gift indeed!

When we got to Joe's house, Harold began to tell him how the previous week his sister and her girlfriend had come to his house. When they entered the room, he said to the girlfriend, "There's something different about your clothes today." She said, "How can you know? You're blind." He started to give us his reply when Joe interrupted and said, " I know what you saw; she wasn't wearing a bra." Whereupon Harold, looking very surprised, said, "How did you know? You weren't there." Then they both broke into laughter. Here were two boys who had, on different occasions, experienced being able to sense when a girl was not wearing a bra, even though they couldn't see her, and now they were witnessing to each other the possibilities of our unlimited minds.

That day I saw Harold's girlfriend taking pictures of him. Later on, as I was talking to Keith, Joe's father, I looked up and couldn't believe my eyes. There was Harold holding a camera and taking a photograph of his girlfriend! (By the way, the photo turned out great.) Shortly after our visit, Joe also began taking photographs, centering the subjects with remarkable accuracy.

Fear Is an Invitation to Peace

I am very thankful for the time I spend with these young teachers because they continually remind me that there are no boundaries we cannot step beyond—a concept I keep mentioning yet somehow keep forgetting. I don't see how it would be possible for anyone to know Tinman, Joe, or Harold without seeing the part that the relinquishment of fear plays in healing.

When viewed correctly, fear can be reinterpreted as our mind's invitation to us to rise to a higher level of freedom. We are not being called to run away from danger but toward safety. And there is a world of difference between these two directions.

Safety lies in "We can." We always choose between that which affirms life and that which merely denies it. Either our thoughts support and lift us upward or they begin sinking us into depression and hopelessness. Even the least of our criticisms or complaints supports an entire belief system that denies the light within each living thing. Our ideas are like the stones on a path we travel. There is not a single thought that does not take us somewhere. That is why we must not leave our minds in a state of fear if we wish to walk toward inner health and peace.

To be free of fear requires only one thing: a goal that is itself not fearful. Trying to change anything is a form of battle. Wanting something that can only be ours in the future blocks our potential to be happy now. Therefore, set for yourself a goal that can be fulfilled where you stand. Make this instant your door to freedom and you will find that it will crack open a little further each time you return to this moment in peace.

Nine
To Give Is to Receive

The third principle of Attitudinal Healing presents the fundamental and universal law of possession. There are few concepts more distrusted than the idea that the only way to keep something of value is to give it away, and conversely, that if we try to take from others, we instantly lose. The third principle states

> *Giving and receiving are the same.* When our attention is on giving and joining with others, fear is removed and we accept healing for ourselves.

Unquestionably our egos believe in the law of scarcity—if we give something to another, we automatically have less. This third principle recognizes that there is another law—a spiritual law—that is based on the truth that we always have an abundance of love. By practicing the third principle, by giving and uniting with others, we activate the law of love.

However, even though the world frequently gives this idea lip service, there is still no widespread belief in it. For example, many girls and boys are given a form of this as advice when they begin dating. Adults are frequently instructed in a more manipulative and indirect version of it in magazines and books that counsel their readers on how to win at the "game" of love and sex.

It was not uncommon in the 1950s for a mother to instruct her daughter who was going out on a date for the first time that she was responsible for putting her date at ease. As a technique, she was advised to act interested in him and not to try to win his attention by talking about herself. Books and magazine articles of the era suggested that she show this interest by asking questions and finding a subject he would enjoy talking about. She wasn't advised to listen with her heart but rather to *act* as if she were listening. Nevertheless, even if she began practicing "giving is receiving" in this somewhat dishonest form, she was still likely to discover how easily she could make herself happy while being thoughtful of her date. She found that as she put her date at ease, she also relaxed.

It isn't that we haven't at times experienced the release from anxiety that comes from giving comfort to others, but we remain convinced that taking and keeping also have their rewards. We make attempts to be patient and kind and then withdraw our love when our efforts are not properly acknowledged. True giving does not require a sacrifice, but a conflicted approach to giving must be looked at honestly if we are ever to know consistent happiness.

We all have had moments when we were caught up in our own problems, whether physical, emotional, or financial, and we were suddenly called upon to help someone in need. Only after the crisis had passed did we notice that our own problems disappeared from our consciousness during the time we were focused on helping another. They disappeared from our awareness, but it is important to note that they may not have disappeared from our life. True healing is not a manipulation of an external situation. It is a change of heart, not a change of circumstances, even though a change of circumstances may accompany it.

When we are centered on giving, we also receive, because our personal anxieties begin to dissipate from our thoughts. When we recognize that what is in the best interests of another is also of complete benefit to us, we gain inner tranquillity, if only briefly, because for that moment we have left our personal hell behind. The mind simply cannot focus on misery when it is flooded with the desire to heal and make happy, even if the forms of misery remain.

Our Focus Is Our Experience

One evening when I was meeting with a new adult group at the Center, I discussed some Attitudinal Healing concepts related to the alleviation of pain. Seated to my left was a woman of about forty named Sarah, who said she had metastatic cancer and had not been free of pain for almost four months, although she was taking large doses of various pain medications.

"Would you be willing to have peace of mind, if only for one instant?" I asked.

"Yes," she responded, "I haven't had peace of mind for years. How do I get it?"

"You have to be willing to look at each person in this room and love them with all the love within you without expecting anything in return," I replied.

She said she was willing, but she seemed a little doubtful. I asked everyone else in the room if they would also focus their full attention on loving Sarah for just one instant. When everyone agreed, I added that none of us would question Sarah about the results. My reason for saying this was that when we evaluate love, we block our awareness of it because confidence is lacking. *Love is a state of trust based on truth.*

When the moment of sharing love was over, the meeting continued as usual. We were saying goodnight a couple of hours later when Sarah suddenly stood up and said, "I can't restrain myself anymore. I have to tell everyone my pain is gone." Then with tears in her eyes, she went around the room and hugged each member of the group.

What Sarah experienced was a joining, through love, with something that had previously appeared to be outside herself. For a moment she experienced the fact that she was not alone. When she was completely involved in extending love, which is her very being, she was not paying attention to her fears about pain. She actually detached herself from pain by detaching herself from her ego image of weakness, vulnerability, isolation, and hopelessness.

What Sarah felt has universal application. The particular form of the physical or psychological distress doesn't matter. In love there is no pain. But it is love we seek and not merely the alleviation of pain.

The term *ego*, as I use it in this book, stands for the mistaken self-concept that we all hold in thought. It is an image or mental picture of ourselves that is completely inaccurate in what it assumes. We are not a thing that is separate and easily hurt. Nor is the reach of our thoughts confined to the boundary of our body. Yet while we focus all our attention on a weak and miserable self-image, as we do most of the time, we block our recognition of what we are. Therefore, we seem to experience all the feelings that a tiny body traveling through a dangerous and uncaring world would experience.

One moment of love, such as the one Sarah experienced, shows us how mistaken our puny self-image can be, for it brings clearly to mind the fact that we are united with all life and that no form of comfort, help, or healing is out of our reach. This cannot be experienced intellectually. Love is essential for this shift in consciousness to be experienced. And it is practical to seek love rather than a worldly solution to our problems, for love does not preclude action; it makes our actions peaceful.

If you begin by trying to experience this kind of love for as long as five minutes, you may not be able to concentrate and your mind may wander off into its usual activity of comparing and judging. And since the practicing of love is identical to the practicing of peace, it would be destructive to make controlling the mind still one more battle. It is freedom from conflict that is the fertile soil from which love so easily sprouts. It would be far better for us to content ourselves with comfort than to add tension to our mental processes in the name of love. A good rule for mental conduct is this: Think whatever thought makes you truly happy.

Once you are successful for one or two seconds, perhaps then you will be encouraged to extend the interval of concentration to several seconds and, later, to a minute or more. As you continue to retrain your mind, you will eventually find that the experience of love and peace can, on occasion, be extended throughout an entire day.

The Help We Give Is Ours to Keep

In just a few moments, my father demonstrated to me that even when we give of our health and strength, the results are not that we have less of them but more. I was having lunch with my parents, who were living in a retirement home, when the following incident occurred.

My father had Parkinson's disease. His symptoms included tremors, difficulty in gait, and a masklike facial expression.

On this day, he also seemed depressed. Sitting with us at the lunch table was a man the same age who was more severely impaired by the same disease than my father. He couldn't walk without help, and when his wife didn't come to assist him, he grew impatient and asked my father to help him to his room.

My father took the man's arm and, with both of them shaking a great deal, they began to walk. Suddenly my father straightened up and his tremor decreased until it was almost invisible. And he began to smile. About ten minutes later he returned. Once again he was walking in a stooped manner.

"What a remarkable demonstration," I thought. When my father was completely absorbed in helping, he was detached from the symptoms of his own helplessness. While he was giving strength and stability, he had noticeably more of both. In addition, he was happy. Once he no longer perceived himself of any use, he returned to a feeble self-concept. And unquestionably all of this happened without his consciously seeing the connection.

Another believer in this cause-and-effect relationship is Paul Johansen, who appeared on *60 Minutes* with Tony Bottarini, another child from the Center. Together they gave the message "teach only love" to over fifty million television viewers. Paul's presence on that program, although unknown to most viewers, was the fulfillment of an agreement he had made with God.

Paul became ill at the age of thirteen and diagnosed himself as having a brain tumor. Subsequent tests proved him right. Later that year, after making out his will, he entered Columbia Presbyterian Hospital in New York City. He was critically ill, had not eaten for a week, and was on intravenous fluids. His family and physician did not expect him to live more than a day or two.

Then a miracle occurred. Here is how Paul later described it to me:

It was in the middle of the night and I didn't know whether I was dreaming or was having a vision or was awake. I do know I was talking to God. I asked God for a flash so I could have a little more time to help my friends. I told Him I was tired of the pain and suffering. I was tired of fighting my cancer. And I was tired of fighting Him. I said to God that I was willing to let His Will be my will, and if I was supposed to die now, that was OK, but I did think I had more to give and I felt He ought to add some extra time. God said he wanted to think about that for a moment. Then He agreed to let me have more time.

The next morning, to everyone's amazement, Paul asked for solid food. In the following days, he began to put on weight and gain strength. Soon, he was able to get into a wheelchair and was discharged from the hospital. Later, he began to walk with a cane and even returned to school.

About this time his mother, Barbara, heard about our program and contacted the Center. Some of the staff and I were scheduled to lecture in New York, and we agreed to meet her for lunch in Manhattan. As we talked, she became enthusiastic about our program and expressed a desire for more contact with us. I told her that I would be back in a few weeks to lecture at Columbia University's College of Physicians and Surgeons on the concepts of life and death and wondered if Paul might be interested in having me interview him as part of the lecture. We decided that Barbara would ask him and that I would phone her later that week.

Paul agreed. We met one hour before the lecture, but it was as if we had known each other all our lives. A correspondent for the local NBC affiliate happened to be filming a story at the hospital that day. He had heard that our interview was about to take place and asked if he could film it. We said, "Yes," and Paul was a brilliant teacher that day as he told his story about his faith in God and how our purpose here on earth is to serve and help each other. Not only was he helpful to a large medical audience, but that night thousands of people were inspired by his courageous spirit on the television broadcast.

A few months later, Paul and his mother came to the Center. He was very excited about going to his first meeting at the Center because he had heard so much about the children. Later, he told his parents that he felt the kids he had met there were more peaceful than any he had ever known.

That night Paul and his mother stayed in my home, and the next morning they attended my regular 9 A.M. prayer meeting. All of us felt the presence of God in a very special way. When we prayed, as was our custom, we simply held hands and were silent. Paul commented, "I like your way of praying where there isn't all that talk." Later that day, he said that he had been "zapped with energy" from the morning's meeting and that he felt better than he had in weeks.

On another occasion, Paul's sister, Kathleen, and I were talking about him before a large audience at Carleton College in Minnesota. When we were through, I suggested that we and the audience spend a few minutes silently sending love to Paul, who was in Connecticut. His parents told me later that at the moment we were praying, Paul felt a rush of energy. He stood up and walked without a cane, something he had not been able to do for months.

This is another example of the healing strength of love and a clear demonstration that minds are not separate. We often forget how strong this silent form of help is. We allow ourselves to slip into a sense of powerlessness because the one who needs us appears distant and unreachable. It is important to remember that the purpose of silently blessing another is not to try to change some physical ailment but to remind ourselves that love is the connecting link between all the children of God. The passing of love from us to another has an unseen effect on a very deep level. The physical effects that Paul experienced are not as important as the love that surrounded him and his family, for this blessing will continue.

The Center kept in frequent telephone contact with Paul and his family. Whenever I was in the East, I would go to Connecticut and visit him. On one of those visits, he was not doing well. He looked pale and depressed. I reminded him that at the Center we believe that sometimes when you are sick, if you will help and love someone, even silently, you can begin to feel happy and your depression will start to disappear. I told him about a new friend of mine, Tony Bottarini, who was ten years old. He had seemed healthy in all respects until a few weeks before when he developed pain in his leg. It turned out to be bone cancer, and he had to have his leg amputated. I said that I was going to be phoning him at the hospital and that perhaps Paul would like to talk with him. I told him I knew he could help.

We placed the call, and once again I saw the phenomenon I have seen so many times. As he began to talk with Tony, this young boy who had looked half dead a few moments earlier became fully alive. He started telling jokes to Tony, and as they talked, a close friendship began to develop between them.

A few weeks later a producer of *60 Minutes* called to say he would like to do a segment on our Center, and he asked me for filmable ideas. I told him that a picture of Tony and Paul talking to each other long-distance would be a powerful demonstration of what young people, completely unassisted, could do for each other.

It occurred to me then that this was part of the fulfillment of God's agreement to give Paul a little more time to help others. However, I don't think Paul ever dreamed that the others would mean over fifty million people.

All during his illness, Paul and his family continued to make presentations with me and to help many other people over the phone. On October 17 at about 5 A.M., I received a phone call from Paul's family telling me he had died peacefully in his sleep. Some years later Tony also died.

Paul's parents and his sister, Kathleen, continue to be dear friends with whom I keep in close contact. I spoke at Kathleen's wedding, and I feel Paul's presence wherever I go. I will always look at Tony and Paul as premiere teachers of love.

Only the Gift of the Heart Matters

The gift we give to others is held within the quiet content of our mind and not just in our words or deeds. The following account, which Sharon Tennison wrote during a sixteen-hour shift with a patient, illustrates the potential strength and beauty of our silent gifts.

> A forty-year-old black male schoolteacher lying quietly in bed . . . a subarachnoid hemorrhage yesterday . . . today he is immobilized, waiting out the bleed in his head. It could abate or blow at any time.
>
> The room is quiet . . . curtains pulled to reduce sensory stimulation . . . vital signs and neuro checks done hourly to monitor his condition . . . ready for any eventuality. The environment is a tense peace, if that is possible.

A little Basque priest making his usual rounds comes in. With real concern he inquires quietly about my patient's condition. I am touched as he walks to the bedrail, holds his hand—palm down—about twelve inches over the man's head, and begins to pray silently. Minutes later he makes a sweeping slow cross over the top part of my patient and quietly fades out of the room. I am aware of tears in my eyes. Why does this touch the heart and soul within me so? This little priest, looking to be in his sixties, salt-and-pepper hair, no taller than five-foot-three, walks around the hospital comforting the grieving, encouraging the sick, and praying with the dying. And here he is today, praying over and loving a sleeping man who doesn't even know him—or know that he is there. And this is his work in the world. He does it with great dignity and compassion.

How many times are there those who are silently holding us in loving thought or prayer when it is completely unknown to us? And I wonder if this might contribute significantly to our life energy. If the scientists and visionaries of the new age are correct, we are linked by a common energy or life force, and the thoughts and energy of one person can affect another.

Which brings me to a haunting possibility—that it does make a difference to every person I am around, or even pass in the hall or on the street, what kind of energy I am emitting. Is it a smile carrying a silent message of love, a quiet acknowledgment that says to them, "I must be worthy. That person thought enough of me to speak?" Or am I throwing out preoccupied energy, keeping in my little mental igloo and encouraging others to do the same? . . . How closed off when I choose the latter . . . how much warmth and understanding when I choose the former.

And my mind slowly comes back from its journey into timeless possibilities, to the bed of this beautiful man, and I take up where the little Basque priest left off and am so touched and humbled by the possibility that we can enter into each other's lives in this silent way.

Our attempts at giving are dissatisfying if we hold back a part of our love or approval at the time we offer our gift. And this holds true no matter what form our gift takes, because the real gift is the extension of the love in our heart. Although our first silent efforts may seem small in light of all that remains to give, even within these efforts we will begin to sense the unlimited treasure within us from which we take. And we will notice another truth: The more we borrow from our store of love and peace, the more abundantly it grows.

The following letter from Marie Van Lint presents a clear example of this beautiful and governing principle of reality. I would like to end this chapter with her letter, so let me make one comment on it now: Marie Van Lint's reward was an inner blessing, not an external one.

I was one of a congregation that overflowed the church. We were there to hear Jerry Jampolsky and others, all very special speakers. The music was beautiful, the feeling vibrant, and I was serenely happy to be there.

The contribution basket was passed around, and I thought, "How much should I put in?" I had received much; now how much should I contribute? As I usually do when I'm not certain of the answer—and often when I am—I referred the matter to the Holy Spirit. "Holy Friend, how much should I give?"

"Everything," came the quiet answer in my mind.

I was startled. "You're kidding," I said. I had just cashed a fair-sized check and the money was in my wallet. "Look, I was thinking in terms of two to five dollars."

"Everything," said the quiet voice.

I opened my wallet and looked. Twenties, tens, fives— my walking-around money for the next two weeks.

"You're sure? All of it?" After all, how could I be sure this was the voice of the Holy Spirit. It could be the voice of ego, of past guilt, of group vibrations; anything.

"Everything."

And I knew I had to go with it. I had always trusted the Voice completely. Not to trust it now meant that I might not trust it for a very long time. There is no such thing as trusting kind of. You trust or you don't.

So I swallowed hard and reached into my wallet, took out the whole wad, and dropped it in the basket. "After all," I thought wryly, "there are still a few coins in the coin purse if I need to feed a parking meter."

"I said everything."

"You really don't let up," I thought as I emptied the few small coins into the basket.

And the most incredible feeling of inner peace and love flooded my heart as the basket passed on. Now I understood that the twenties, the tens, would have been meaningless without the last few coins and that the lesson had nothing at all to do with money.

It was commitment. Total commitment. I could travel light years toward my goal, but if I stopped an inch short of it, all the miles would be useless.

That is the gift that was given me. To give all is to receive all. It may seem, on the face of it, that the exchange was totally unequal—spiritual awareness in exchange for some dollars—but I think otherwise. To give the Holy Spirit an instant—The Holy Instant—of absolute trust and commitment is the gift He asks for. It is a great and worthy gift and it is what I had to give. That His gifts to me are so much greater doesn't matter. They are what He has to give.

Ten

Releasing the Past and the Future

The fourth principle of Attitudinal Healing is the key that opens the door to Love's presence and allows us to see ourselves and others with eyes that reflect peace and oneness. This principle states

> *We can let go of the past and the future.* We experience inner peace when we let go of our attachments to the painful past and the fearful future and learn to live in the present.

At the Center we are convinced that a major reason for much of the weariness, anger, and depression that so many people experience comes from a preoccupation with the past. When our minds are focused on old wounds and unforgiving thoughts about our past, it's no wonder we feel overburdened by the present. We are carrying the weight of the past with us, and our bodies and minds reflect this.

Burnout

Both at work and at home, too many of us feel burned-out and exhausted much of the time. We tend to blame this on the stress of our jobs or the problems in our families, but the truth is that most of our disillusionment and weariness is caused by the judgments we have against ourselves and others. These judgments have their roots in our unforgiven past, and unfortunately they poison our capacity to experience directly what is occurring here and now. Clearly this undercuts our ability to relax and enjoy our lives.

It Is Our Mind, Not Our Body

At the Center we know that healing takes place first in the mind. Attitudinal Healing focuses on the mind as the "control center" of our sense of physical well-being, emotional wholeness, and ability to perceive clearly and communicate meaningfully.

The importance of our attitude can be seen in an experience most of us are familiar with. We arrive home from work after a particularly difficult day. Our body is moving slowly, our spirits are lagging, and all we can contemplate is eating a quick dinner and collapsing into bed. Suddenly the phone rings, and it's a dear friend who's in town for the night and wants to meet for dinner. "I'll be there in an hour," we say.

Whistling with joy, we jump in the shower and suddenly are full of energy. What happened? The day didn't change. Nothing happened to our body. But our attitude underwent a transformation because we shifted from being preoccupied with the past (our exhausting day) to focusing on the present (preparing to be with our friend). When we were responding from the past, we felt drained of energy. When we responded from the present, we were joyful and full of energy.

Fear of the Future

Our fear of the future comes from the belief that the past is going to repeat itself in some painful way. When we continue to think of ourselves as damaged by our past, we must view the future fearfully because we believe more strongly in rejection and pain than we do in love and oneness. With this attitude, it is almost impossible to be happy.

Many of us spend so much time brooding about the past and being afraid of the future that we do not even live in the here and now. Indeed, we superimpose the past upon the present and taint all of our experiences with old, unhappy lessons. How can we view our future with anything but dread when this is our attitude?

This point was made wonderfully clear to me one day when I was driving my rather old Honda. I went over a small bump and the rearview mirror broke off and fell to the floor. Recognizing that this was a rather peculiar event, I pulled over to the side of the road to meditate about what it might mean. A few minutes later I burst out laughing at the answer I had received.

"Jerry," my inner voice asked, "when are you going to stop looking backwards as you go through life?"

It has been my good fortune to meet many people who have chosen not to see themselves as victims of the past and therefore do not impose the past upon the present. A good illustration is the man who recently drove me from Hollywood to Costa Mesa, California, where I was to give a speech.

As we drove, we began to talk, and he eventually told me a little of his life story. He had been born in Italy, and for as long as he could remember, he was obsessed with making a lot of money. After moving to the United States, he had become quite successful in the jewelry business and was indeed making a great deal of money. He said that ten years ago he had taken a buying trip to Europe and had returned to Los Angeles International Airport with over two million dollars worth of jewelry in a suitcase. After going through customs at the airport, he had carried his merchandise to his car.

About ten minutes after leaving the airport, his tire suddenly blew out, and he swerved to the side of the road. As he opened his door to get out of the car, a man pointed a gun at his head and demanded the suitcase. The thief had obviously followed him and had put a bullet into his tire.

The police were never able to find the thief or the jewelry. Needless to say, this man was filled with remorse and harshly blamed himself for being so stupid and careless. As a result of the theft, he lost his business and felt that his life was ruined. He became depressed and could not forgive himself for what he had done.

About a year after the theft he visited his mother in Italy, and she reminded him that when he was a child during World War II, their family had lost everything because they were Jewish. She emphasized that the family had learned that what was truly important in life was not the money and the possessions they had lost but the love they had for each other. This love could neither be taken from them nor lost, and it alone carried them through those dark days. On the flight back to the United States, he recognized that his mother was right and that her wisdom was all he needed to be able to forgive himself and let go of the past.

For nine years he has been driving for the same company, and he discovered that he loves this work. He meets many different kinds of people, some of whom confide in him, and he often finds himself in a position to help. The lifestyle of his family is quite different, but they are happier than they have ever been. They have enough money to meet their needs, and he has found a new purpose in life that has brought him the kind of fulfillment he never experienced before. He lives in the present and offers his love and his help to those whose lives he touches. The past has no more meaning for him because he has found love and peace in the present.

On another occasion Diane and I flew to Boston to speak at a conference on healing and laughter. We were picked up at the airport by two clowns! One of the clowns was a sixty-seven-year-old man with a fascinating story that he shared with us.

A year and a half before, he had lost his life savings on the stock market. He was devastated and felt that his life was hopeless and that he was a complete failure. He continued to flounder in the quicksand of the past until a friend finally convinced him to attend a night class so that they could learn to be clowns. He was extremely resistant but finally agreed to go. Becoming a clown allowed him to release his past and extend love and healing in the present—to himself and others.

He told us that he now spends almost all of his "clown" time visiting children in pediatric wards of hospitals, and his life now is more fun, exciting, and fulfilling than he had ever imagined it could be. Again, this is another person who chose to stop being a victim of the past and learned to live in the present.

One of the greatest gifts we can give ourselves is to decide that we are no longer willing to remain stuck in the past or to be fearful of the future. Much of our focus at the Center involves actively releasing the past through the conscious recognition that we can free our minds by choosing to forgive everyone we believe has injured us. This happy work then allows us to place our future in the hands of God.

Eleven
Why Not Now?

The present is the only time we can choose between love and fear. When we fret about the past or worry about what to do in the future, we accomplish nothing. And yet, our mental habit of reliving the past and rehearsing what is to come generates various forms of pain. A mental shift back into the present helps remove the source of misery. The fifth principle of Attitudinal Healing states

> *Now is the only time there is.* Pain, grief, depression, guilt, and other forms of fear disappear when the mind is focused in loving peace on this instant.

This principle suggests another reality that is not based on linear time but rather on an instant of timelessness that can be eternally extended. It is possible to live each second within such timelessness and to experience the loving calm that awaits only our decision to focus on giving unconditional love to each other now. In this holy moment there are no expectations, no assumptions, and no confusions. We are at home in peace.

Recovering the Present

There is usually a tremendous preoccupation with the past and future when we are suffering from illness or pain. We are tempted to look at all our past miseries and wonder how long we will have to endure this. When we are ill and hurting, it often feels as if no one loves us. To the contrary, it feels as if we are being punished or in some other way attacked for something we suspect is our fault. Consequently, we may spend most of our time focused on our body, measuring the sickness and pain, wondering what we did to deserve this, and predicting that the next moment will surely be like the last. And, of course, we tend to prove these predictions right.

As I have stated often in this book, I have been impressed with how quickly pain can disappear when we direct our mind outside ourselves in a caring way to others. This care or joining can be in our willingness to receive love as well as our willingness to give direct help to another. Randy Romero's story is a wonderful example. He was a twenty-five-year-old who was hospitalized with cancer. His pain was difficult to control even though he was on high doses of morphine (over 100 mg. hourly). He had been very active in sports and had helped children at our Center in a project that allowed them to meet famous sports figures.

Shortly before he died, I asked Randy, "Of all the people you have heard about in sports, what person would you like to meet most of all, if it were possible?" He replied, "Bernard King." Randy admired him not only for his excellence as an athlete but because he had whipped a drug problem and now was helping others.

I didn't know anyone in the Golden State Warriors office, but I phoned anyway. The results came quickly. By 2:30 the next afternoon, Bernard King was visiting Randy, who transformed from someone bedridden and immobilized with pain into a young man filled with enthusiasm. He had his photograph taken with Bernard and they talked about drugs and laughed together as they walked down the hall in each other's arms. Randy had no pain during those two and a half hours, and later his mother told me that he said it had been one of the happiest days of his life. He died peacefully two weeks later.

There is much we can do for others, and for that very reason, there is much we can do for ourselves. Randy and Bernard experienced love simply because they gave so much of it. In the process, fear and pain disappeared. If it is true that only now is real, then the past cannot hurt us, and it will not hurt us unless we make it a part of our present. The mind can always be used to love rather than to make one more sad review of what is already finished. Let bygones be bygones; let love be now.

Guilt Is a Denial of the Present

Our present thoughts and choices are the sole determiner of our present experience. Because this statement is so foreign to how we usually approach life, I would like to give you an illustration from my own life.

One day while brushing my teeth, I sneezed. My back went into acute spasm and I fell to the floor, screaming in agony. I was hospitalized, had many examinations, and was told I had "organic back syndrome." I was put in traction and given drugs. Two weeks later, I left the hospital feeling better but still in pain. For the next five years I don't think I was ever free of it. My physician advised me to stop all physical exercise—tennis, basketball, jogging, skiing, gardening—which were all activities I loved.

As the years went by, the chronic nature of my condition became increasingly apparent. I was simply going to have to learn to adapt myself to this disability. Surgery might be helpful, but there was no guarantee.

Later, I began to notice that my back seemed to be a barometer of even the slightest emotional stress. But I tricked myself into believing that my reaction to stress was not a fundamental cause of the pain because I possessed x-rays which showed that my condition was organically caused. At one point my back became so bad that I was hospitalized again. The consulting neurosurgeon strongly recommended surgery. He went so far as to predict that without it my pain would never disappear. As I was facing that decision, I suddenly saw the truth, which had been there all the time.

I realized that behind my back pain was a complex of thoughts which included anger, resentment, fear, and guilt, all of which were my personal ties to the past. These feelings appeared to be caused by long-standing conflicts in my first marriage. I saw that I was angry at my wife for not supplying what I felt I lacked and for not meeting my needs. And yet I was also feeling guilty about having such angry thoughts about her and believed I deserved to be punished for them. The back pain also gave me an excuse to drink more when the drugs were not effective. I decided that I would try to undo the cause of the pain in another way rather than undergo surgery.

I am not saying that surgery is either right or wrong. My decision to forego it at that time was simply the one I personally needed to refocus my mind. The body, by itself, is not what is important. Therefore, we must do whatever allows us to let go of our preoccupation with it and return to peace. It is the goal of peace that will indicate how to care for our body this instant. We should simply do what the aim of sustaining and deepening our inner happiness dictates. Such an approach is far superior to making rigid decisions about the future, which merely tempt us to consult past decisions and fears rather than our peaceful preference at the moment.

As a result of these new insights and my determination to pursue them, my back problems improved but did not go away. After my divorce, I found that the stresses of other circumstances and relationships were also displaced onto my body. One weekend, years later, I was almost hospitalized because of an acute attack. It was a classic example of how guilt manifests itself in the most symbolic part of our body.

I was attending a conference in Virginia, where I met a very attractive and intelligent woman. We immediately became intimately involved. It felt like two lost souls finding each other. But my newfound friend turned out to be married, and I very quickly began experiencing tremendous feelings of guilt.

After the conference she invited me to have dinner with her and her husband the next time I came to New York. In my state of rising guilt, meeting her husband was the last thing I wanted to do. Yet another part of me yearned to be with her one more time, so I changed my original plans and flew to New York.

As I picked up my suitcase at Kennedy Airport, an acute pain shot through my back and I collapsed. I managed to get to the airport bar, where I had more than a few drinks. Later, I got a taxi and went to my hotel. Severe back spasms continued, and I returned to San Francisco the next day in agony. It was a full month before I was free of pain.

After I was introduced to *A Course in Miracles*, I began to realize how attached to guilt I was. I became aware that this attachment caused me to fear love, which is the same thing as fearing the present. Many of you may assume that I should have felt guilty since I had had an affair with a married woman. But guilt can't alter our past behavior or cause us to treat others more lovingly.

As I learned to let go of guilt and anxiety, I experienced a new sense of well-being. I decided that as best I could I would no longer allow myself to be limited by my judgments of the past and my fears of the future. But I saw that I couldn't do this alone; I had to ask God's help in making such a radical break with what had become my habitual way of thinking.

I am now actively involved in physical activities that I once was told I would never be able to participate in. However, I want you to know that I am not consistent in practicing these spiritual principles. There are many times I am tempted to judge and to make fearful decisions about the future. When I do, and when my mind is not in harmony, I will sometimes feel tension in my back. Then I look for the unforgiving thought beneath the pain. I quiet my mind and tell myself I want the peace of God more than anything else. I pray, asking my inner Teacher for help in forgiving, and I give thanks that I am joined to everyone in love. When I do this, I often find that the back tension disappears, but more importantly, I again feel God's loving and constant presence.

Now Is Another Name for Love

It might be helpful to examine the mental process behind my episodes of back pain a little more closely. Back pain itself is very common in our society, and yet all physical pain is produced in a similar way, and likewise, its remedy is basically the same.

The fifth principle of Attitudinal Healing links freedom from pain with awareness of the present. Certainly we all think we are aware of the present, and it is true that most of us do see the objects and hear the sounds that surround us. But notice that the fifth principle states that pain and other forms of fear disappear only when the mind is focused *in love* on this instant. If we are using the people around us only as a means of recalling the past, we can hardly claim to be focusing our loving attention on them or on the present.

It was a small step in the right direction for me to associate my back pain with my judgmental attitudes toward my first wife rather than with only a deteriorated disk, but it was a mistake for me to believe that the years of conflict within our marriage were somehow responsible for my present anger and pain. Guilt produces projection, and projection is simply a way of shifting blame to another rather than releasing blame. And because projection is a form of attack, it makes us feel even more guilty, and so we continue punishing ourselves in some way.

If we see people as they are now, we are currently practicing forgiveness. But if looking at them is only our excuse for recalling their past mistakes, then they become a means for hurting. Our new practice should be the consistent cleansing of our vision of all past associations. We must constantly free all we see of negative and limiting memories.

The cycle of feeling guilty, shifting blame to others, getting angry at the guilt we now see in them, attacking them for their guilt, feeling even more guilty for our attack, and finally punishing our bodies in payment cannot be escaped as long as we believe that guilt is a valid description of anything meaningful. We must make a decision for innocence if we are ever to have consistent mental peace and the resulting bodily peace.

The innocence of others cannot be found in their past behavior. This innocence may also be hard to see within their present behavior. But it can be found in the peace that is within *us*. It is viewed beyond the personality, beyond bodily behavior, and beyond our mental associations. It is like a light that shines within our heart and the heart of the other person. Once it is glimpsed, it is far more real to us than guilt, because it *is* more real. All we need to do in order to free ourselves of pain, grief, depression, guilt, and other forms of fear is to undertake the search for innocence.

Several months ago, I was asked to see a woman in her late fifties who had cancer of the brain. When I arrived at her home, I first spent some time with her husband, Ed. He told me his family had been fortunate because no one had ever been seriously ill prior to this, so it was quite a shock when his wife was diagnosed with cancer. She had been operated on but the cancer was not removable. Despite chemotherapy and x-ray treatment, the prognosis was guarded.

Ed said he had come from a poor family with many children. When he was seven years old there wasn't enough food to feed everyone, and he pledged to himself that when he grew up this would never happen to his family. As a young man, he went into business for himself, worked long hours, and was rarely home. His wife had raised their two children largely by herself. Ed became quite wealthy. His son joined him in the business, and life seemed satisfactory until his wife became ill. When that happened, for the first time in their marriage he decided to spend more time at home.

One day their gardener said to him, "One of the rosebushes in the garden looks like it has died. Is it all right if I pull it out and replace it?" Ed thought a moment and then said he would like to see it. As he stood looking down at the bush, it occurred to him that he had one of the loveliest rose gardens in the city, yet in the last twenty years he had never taken time to enjoy it.

"Don't pull it out. It is alive, and I would like to care for it myself," he said. Daily, Ed visited the garden to love, nourish, and water the rosebush. It began to come back to life, and several weeks later a beautiful rose appeared. Ed snipped it off and took it to his wife, whose name, of course, was Rose.

Because of how he chose to respond to his wife's illness, Ed was now able to realize how much of life he had let pass him by. He had been so preoccupied with accumulating more money for the future that he had forgotten to live in the present.

After hearing that surprising story, I talked to Rose. I asked what had been going on in her life before she developed cancer; for example, had there been any stress preceding the onset? She said no, she and her husband and children had been perfectly happy. A few minutes later, however, tears came to her eyes, and she shared some significant information. When Ed first went into business twenty-five years ago, her brother became his partner. The following year, Ed bought her brother's share of the business, but the brother felt he had not received enough money in the financial arrangement and hadn't spoken to either Ed or her since.

Rose stated that she loved both her brother and husband but felt loyalty to her husband. Through the intervening years, she had a nagging sense of guilt that she should resolve the conflict. She was depressed about the situation but had never talked about it until now. I explained to her how important I thought it was for her to resolve this. Otherwise, she might have some ambivalence about ever being happy again because she knew she would still have to face a life situation that she found painful. We talked about forgiveness, not only between her brother and her husband but also for herself. She gave me permission to bring Ed in and speak with both of them about it.

It was difficult for Ed to believe that the wife he knew so well had kept this from him while feeling such conflict for all these years. He immediately went to the phone to call her brother to ask forgiveness. The next day there was a reconciliation.

Rose, like Ed, had not been living in the present, even though the way they had avoided it had taken different forms.

Their joint recognition of the beauty and harmony always inherent in the living moment, allowed their relationship to bloom, and for the remaining months that Rose lived, they were immeasurably happier.

Nothing Is Required to Be Here Now

To live peacefully and happily in the present is so very simple that when we first become aware of it, we stand in disbelief at all we have put ourselves through before. How easy it is to forget the past and future and be content now! What do we do that makes it all so difficult? Here are three common ways we add unnecessary complication to our lives, along with suggestions on how to return to simplicity and peace:

1. *If we fear the world, we will be hesitant to do anything without considering all the consequences.* Since it is impossible to move even a chair without ramifications, anxiety accompanies even the smallest events of each day. How simple it is to acknowledge that we are not in a position to see the outcome of anything and that all the worry in the world cannot control the future. How simple it is to see that we can only be happy now and that there will never be a time when it is not now. We endlessly complicate our lives when our focus is on results. It is only our effort that we can control. Success lies in how we try and not in our or other people's appraisal of the effect. If we would take just half the time we spend worrying about ramifications and use it instead on direct action, nothing important would go undone. Simplicity lies in putting effort before results.

2. *As a baby struggles to learn to walk, she never pauses to analyze why she just fell down.* With each fall, an adjustment is automatically made. The baby instinctively knows that she

is being taught and never tries to teach herself lessons she does not understand. Adults, on the other hand, spend a remarkable portion of their lives going over and over each mistake in a vain attempt to categorize what has in fact already been internally assimilated. How simple it is to resign as our own teacher. How easy it can be to turn quickly from the past, because the present is where our life is taking place.

3. *Learning to respond to now is all there is to learn, and we are not responding to this instant if we are judging any aspect of it.* The ego looks around for something to criticize. This always involves a comparison with the past. But love looks upon the world peacefully and accepts. The ego searches for shortcomings and weaknesses. Love watches for any sign of light and strength. It sees how far we have come and not how far we have to go. How simple it is to love and how exhausting it is to always find fault, for every time we see a fault we think something needs to be done about it. Love knows that nothing is ever needed but more love.

Twelve

Learning to Love, Learning to Forgive

Forgiveness is the means whereby we experience peace, know ourselves as love, give without sacrifice, join with the essence of others, experience fully this instant, and hear clearly the inner counseling of happiness. Forgiveness is the way all the rules of Attitudinal Healing are understood and applied. The sixth principle is

> *We can learn to love ourselves and others by forgiving rather than judging.* Forgiveness is the way to true health and happiness. When we choose to see everyone as a teacher of forgiveness, each moment gives us an opportunity for happiness, peace, and love.

Forgiveness allows us to release the past and let go of our fears of the future. In so doing, we experience the truth that everyone is our teacher and that each situation is new and therefore full of potential.

Because we tend to project our own anger onto others, the effect of forgiving others instantly allows us to forgive ourselves. This is the experience of oneness because we are reminded that the essence of our being is Love.

Our egos are constantly judgmental—either condemning others or attacking ourselves. Unfortunately many of us firmly believe that some people commit unforgivable acts and that our safety lies in never forgiving or forgetting those we believe have injured us. This belief serves only to destroy our peace of mind and often our health as well.

What Is Forgiveness?

In this book I do not use the word *forgiveness* the way it is often used. Here, it does not mean that we repress our anger and act as if everything is acceptable when we are clearly feeling that it isn't. Nor, of course, does it mean that we act out our anger. And above all, it does not mean that we assume a position of superiority and pardon sins that we believe are real.

To forgive does not mean we must remarry our ex-spouse, let prisoners out of jails, return to our old job, or anything else overt. The ego believes that if it forgives the one who has harmed it, it must translate this forgiveness into some behavior. But true forgiveness requires no bodily action, even though some gesture may perhaps accompany it. Forgiveness is an inner correction that lightens our heart and frees us to live in the present. It is for our peace of mind first. Being at peace, we now have peace to extend to others, and this is the most permanent and valuable gift we can possibly give.

The root meaning of the verb *to forgive* is "to let go." Forgiveness is relinquishing an unhelpful train of thought; it is giving back to the ego that which we now recognize as undesirable. Forgiveness is the gentle refusal to defend ourselves against love. It sees that all things are forgivable. It is a willingness to perceive everyone, including ourselves, as either expressing love or feeling a need for love. Any form of attack is a call for help, and the answer to every call for help is gentleness.

Forgiveness, like every other spiritual quality I have mentioned in this book—peace, love, equality, innocence, fearlessness, stillness, joy—does not imply a type of behavior. For example, to be *peaceful* does not imply that we must become docile; to be *loving* does not require that we adopt certain mannerisms and a particular tone of voice; to recognize our spiritual *equality* with others does not mean it is desirable to lower ourselves to their ego level; to see our own *guiltlessness* is not to continue repeating past mistakes; to be *fearless* we do not have to place ourselves or others in danger; to practice mental *quietness* we need not react to the world by fleeing from it; and to be *happy* does not mean we turn instead to an anxious form of ego excitement. Likewise, practicing forgiveness does not imply that we must tell people we forgive them or act "holier than thou" around them. In Attitudinal Healing, the changing of our attitudes may result in certain changes in the way we act, but we usually recognize them in retrospect, and we never make modifying our behavior our first priority.

This may appear to contradict an earlier statement I made that after pausing in peace we should act with assurance. But to say that it is better to do all we do in confidence is not to specify what action should be taken confidently. It is also better to act from love and peace, yet this must apply to all activities. Any decision made and carried out in the spirit of true forgiveness will bless everyone it touches and will not harm anyone.

Mother Teresa was always an inspiration to me. Her words and example supplied me with a gentle and needed correction on more than one occasion, and without knowing it, she once taught me an important lesson. The stand she took at the Transpersonal Association Conference in India was a clear and loving example of true forgiveness.

The conference was on the general theme of world peace, and one of the speakers circulated a statement opposing the nuclear-arms race and asked the other speakers if they would sign. I agreed to, as did a number of the others. But when Mother Teresa was asked, she prayed and then answered that she would not be able to. "If I signed," she said, "I would be loving some people and not others because I would be taking sides in a controversy."

True forgiveness is based on reality. It overlooks the evidence gathered from the point of view of a single body and turns instead to the universal truth of our reality—that each of us is innocent and loved completely by God. It's not that we haven't made countless mistakes and will probably continue to do so for some time. But true forgiveness distinguishes between the deep urges of the heart and the more superficial desires of the ego. All mistakes come from the ego and are part of the learning process that everyone must go through. Forgiveness is a gentle vision that sees the maturity, the goodness of heart, and the wholeness of character that will come in time to each person. And it recognizes the inappropriateness of condemnation to this growth process.

Intolerance Is a Failure to See

It is not just people we must forgive. Grievances can be held against cities, certain animals, a particular season of the year, foods, styles of dress; in fact, anything the body's eyes see can become a source of unhappiness and even pain if we are intolerant of it. When Sharon Winter first came to the Center, she was seventeen. Like many children, she had sensed the gravity of her condition before her doctor made his diagnosis. Her opinion had not been taken seriously, and Sharon had gone untreated for over a year before new tests were ordered and the cancerous condition known as lymphosarcoma was discovered. For this and several other reasons, by the time she reached our Center she was very angry with the medical establishment and was suspicious of us.

At the time of her first visit, we had just one group of children, starting at age five. Sharon really didn't think she could learn anything from young kids, although at her first meeting she was surprised to see how happy everyone was. She suspected that even this was put on for her benefit. What amazed her most, however, was that an eight-year-old girl named Andrea, who had leukemia, was able to help her deal with her fear of an upcoming bone-marrow procedure. Andrea suggested that Sharon could take her mind completely off it by picturing herself on a beach in Hawaii, basking in the sun. She added, "You have to imagine it like you believe it one hundred percent." Sharon later did exactly as her young teacher instructed, and to her amazement her fear and pain were minimal.

Mental Imagery

Before I continue with Sharon's story, I would like to expand a little on how mental imagery works, because there are many who might read the above paragraph and think that what Andrea said was so childish and overly simplistic as to be virtually useless to adults. Unfortunately, this is often true—not because mental-imagery games are ineffective but because most adults will not allow themselves to try such a simple and direct approach.

Anything that can be stated as a concept can also be acted out in the imagination. Forgiveness, for example, is the exercise of our capacity to forget. We forget it because it is not worth thinking about. We forget it because to continue to remember it weakens us and makes us miserable. For many, a mental image, such as the one I suggest in *Love Is Letting Go of Fear*, of filling a garbage can with our problems, attaching a helium balloon, and watching it all float out of sight can allow the mind to concentrate a little longer and thereby go a little deeper. A simple imagery such as imagining the light of God shining down upon the pain or the event, watching it surround it and dissolve it until there is nothing left but this light, can do much to release the mind of distress. The power is not in the particular imagery used but in our willingness to do something now to regain our peace.

As the months went by, Sharon went into remission, grew her hair back, recommenced her education, and eventually fell in love with a fine young man whom she later married. However, after we all thought that everything was going so well for her, at the age of twenty-one, Sharon suffered a recurrence of cancer. Her faith in her doctor, the world, and God was severely shaken. All her old anger toward the medical establishment returned as she faced multiple tests, new chemotherapy, losing her hair, and most of all the uncertainty of the outcome.

She finally agreed to return to the hospital she so hated to resume treatment. On the day of her scheduled discharge, she was eager to go home. But that morning, a fifteen-year-old girl entered the hospital and was put in the bed next to Sharon. The girl's story was a most pathetic one. She had been abandoned by her parents and was going from one friend's home to another. Although suffering from Hodgkin's disease, she was terrified about the aftereffects of chemotherapy and hadn't made up her mind whether to stay in the hospital or sign herself out.

Despite her personal eagerness to leave now that her own treatment series was over, Sharon decided to stay an extra day as if nothing had happened, just so she could be there to help this new young friend. When her doctor discovered she had not checked out, he came into her room and asked her what was going on. When she told him the story, she saw her doctor cry for the first time.

Intolerance, even intolerance of institutions such as hospitals, police departments, school administrations, and government bureaus, is a failure to see beyond appearances. It is a thought drawn from the past and imposed on what is presently being seen and usually has little to do with what is taking place this instant. Sharon's concern for this young girl allowed her to see the situation clearly and to set aside her own needs and to act from love.

Forgiveness Is a Seeing Calmly

Intolerance, like all loveless feelings—fear, impatience, jealousy, anger, depression, and so on—does not need to be fought or even resisted. The purpose of Attitudinal Healing is not to make the mind a battlefield. To add one more grudging obligation to our life—the obligation to forgive—is to fail completely to understand that forgiveness is our door to happiness.

Negative feelings evaporate whenever they are looked at calmly and honestly. This process is often gradual. All that is needed is that a gentle *effort* to forgive be made whenever we sense the willingness to make such an attempt. Once we experience the blessing this brings our own mind, these efforts become a pleasure.

Any emotion or thought that distresses us will begin to lose its hold on the mind when it is examined peacefully. Behind every negative feeling is an ego request, and we do not need to be afraid to look at what we are being asked to do, for when we see clearly what is being demanded by our ego, we also see that we do not want to do it.

A good habit to cultivate is to pause whenever you are having difficulty releasing your mind from an upset and look directly and in detail at the contents of your mind. Only a fearful avoidance of your attack thoughts will appear to give them power over you. Nothing negative can stand before the light of peace. But do not make the mistake of getting caught up in analyzing the contents of your mind. For example, it will waste your time and will probably depress you to ask yourself why you started feeling this way, how long has it gone on, why do you keep making this same mistake, and what rule can you make to avoid feeling this way in the future.

Instead, just look calmly at your unforgiving thoughts, in whatever form they are presently taking, and hear them out. Let your fears tell you their insane tale about the future. Allow your anger to suggest its ridiculous course of action. If you do this quietly and honestly, you will eventually laugh happily at the absurdity of it all and proceed again in love. There is no destructive thought or feeling that can withstand a persistent awareness.

I remember when we began working with a family who had a son, twelve years of age, who had brain cancer. From all appearances, he did not have much longer to live. One day, the boy's father called me and said he had been dismissed from his job, not for negligence, but because of a companywide reorganization. He was furious at the company's insensitivity, for they were all aware of his son's illness. Now he was being forced to go out on interviews, and this was upsetting him not only because it was taking him away from his son but also because the people who were interviewing him were much younger and less experienced than he was. He asked me for any thought that might help.

I told him that if he wanted peace of mind, it was important to forgive the people where he had worked and also important to see that those who were interviewing him were not his enemies. He had told me that he had another appointment for the next day, and I suggested that this time he look calmly at the young interviewer who would be questioning him and see that he too was nervous. The interviewer would naturally be afraid of overlooking something and getting the wrong person for the job. If the one he hired did not work out, this could possibly jeopardize his own position. I told him that once he saw for himself that the interviewer was also scared he would understand that they had come together to bring each other peace, even if the interviewer did not recognize this. I suggested that he set a single goal—not to get the job but to have peace of mind during the interview by extending his love and consideration to the interviewer.

He called me back the next night and said, "You know, Jerry, I don't have any idea whether they will take me, but I do know I felt better when I left that interview than I have felt in a long, long time." As it turned out, he did get the job—and at a higher salary than his previous position. This, of course, is not what is important, because learning to practice the healing power of forgiveness cannot be compared to any other benefit in this life.

Forgiveness is unquestionably the concept most central to Attitudinal Healing, and yet it is also the one most likely to be misunderstood. I have already said that true forgiveness is not the adoption of a morally superior position. Nor does it acknowledge someone else's cruelty and pronounce it acceptable, for to do this would be dishonest. Forgiveness sees that no real grounds for condemnation exist, and for that to happen, new grounds for innocence must be recognized. Certainly the person's behavior cannot be rationalized away. He did behave the way he behaved. Possibly another motivation can be attributed to his behavior, such as fear instead of selfishness, and although this can be a good first step, it is not sufficient in itself to allow us to see the splendor of God's light within him. Forgiveness is a gentle turning away from what we see with our body's eyes and searching for the truth that lies beyond the individual's ego.

Most people understand that deep urges for goodness exist in everyone's heart no matter how obscured they may be with guilt, defensiveness, dishonesty, and inhumanity. Forgiveness looks beyond the more superficial motivations of individuals, no matter how extreme these may be, to the place in their heart where they yearn for exactly what we yearn for. Everyone wants peace and safety. Everyone wants to make a difference. And everyone wants to release their potential for love. It is deep into this desire that forgiveness gazes, and seeing there a reflection of itself, it releases the person from judgment.

$\mathcal{T}hirteen$
Becoming Love-Finders

The seventh principle of Attitudinal Healing presents a clear choice we must all eventually make if we wish to know lasting peace and love. This choice requires a shift in perception from looking at the appearance or behavior of others to seeing the innocent heart we all share. Once made, this shift brings us nothing less than the experience of Heaven. It states

We can become love-finders rather than faultfinders. Regardless of what another person's behavior may be, we can always choose to see only the light of love in that person.

All egos are alike. One ego is not better than another, and once we understand this and recognize how our ego operates, we can choose to react from our peaceful mind, our happy mind, our connected mind.

The ego is like an automatic pilot that can take us in only one direction—toward judgment, anger, fear, and guilt. Some people may act this out more destructively than others, but the fundamental mistake is the same. Very simply, the ego is a "faultfinder," and it doesn't care who or what is the object of its unhappy focus. The result is always the same—when we respond from the ego we have no sense of unity or wholeness within ourselves or our relationships, and we cannot experience peace of mind.

To sustain inner peace, we must let go of our faultfinding judgments and instead become love-finders.

Walking along the Beach

My wife, Diane, and I love to take long walks on beaches. Sometimes we are silent and meditative. Other times we talk to each other. But always we try to look at everything we see with love—the waves, the clouds, and especially the people we meet along the way.

In days past I used to focus judgmentally on the people who had the biggest bellies. Today, however, that kind of looking does not even occur to me because I am focused on recognizing the tender heart full of love that we all share. I do not become preoccupied with appearances or whether people seem sad or happy, angry or contented, friendly or unfriendly.

During some walks Diane and I smile at everyone who passes and say "Good morning" or "Good afternoon." Many respond with a smile and a greeting, and others do not. We understand that it is not the response, or lack of one, which matters. We simply know that we will experience more peace and joy if we greet everyone we see with love.

Marriage

Relationships in which both partners are focused on each other's faults quickly deteriorate, because neither partner can do anything right. Conflict and strife are the result of looking at each other in this way. When Diane and I counsel couples, before they begin to talk about their problems, we ask them to first say a few positive things about each other. Often they have tremendous resistance to this suggestion, and sometimes neither can think of a single, loving thing to say about the other.

Sometimes they are disappointed with Diane and me because they had looked forward to, and perhaps even silently rehearsed, relating their long lists of complaints along with the obvious conclusion that their partner is to blame for everything that is wrong in the marriage.

Sooner or later one of them will venture a tentative, "Well, I guess she does try to be a good and loving mother." The other might then respond, "It's kind of him to phone me and let me know that he's coming home late." This breaks the ice of negativity, and with very little encouragement from us, they begin coming up with very different lists—ones that acknowledge goodness, thoughtfulness, and love. The hostile energy begins to dissipate, and soon one of them will say, with tenderness and surprise, "I've never heard you say that before. I didn't know you thought that."

Please notice that nothing has changed in their relationship except their attitudes. They have turned from faultfinding to love-finding. We then can go on to discuss specific issues, but now both individuals are willing to listen to each other without defensiveness or anger. Possible solutions and ideas for strengthening their relationship now come quickly and easily to their minds. Becoming a "love-finder" is practical, and it works!

Mirroring

Most of us have a list of things that we don't like or accept about ourselves. Most of us have also acted in ways that we are ashamed of or embarrassed about. But instead of forgiving ourselves and healing these sore places in our minds, our egos cleverly project these "faults" and "mistakes" onto others, as if seeing another as guilty makes us innocent. It is very difficult to believe that what we criticize or dislike in another is often a reflection of what we have rejected in ourselves.

We may see someone else as racially prejudiced but not want to look at the part of us that is not free of prejudice. The ego actually believes that we can prove our innocence by making someone else guilty. We may call another person narrow-minded while denying our own narrow way of thinking.

Because our egos believe in separation, they tempt us to go through the day looking for blemishes in each other. This way of looking often seems automatic until we begin to question its validity and its effect on us and our relationships.

Becoming a Love-Finder

Those who honestly monitor their thoughts are usually appalled to discover how many of them are negative and judgmental. But our egos don't want us to be aware of this, because they desire conflict, separation, and fear. It is painful to realize that there is a part of all of us that wants nothing more than our unhappiness. But this recognition, rather than proving our guilt, allows us to look beyond the ego to our deeper self, our connected self, our loving self. Very simply, the way to inner peace is to go beyond faultfinding and to become love-finders.

Once we make the decision to go through life loving rather than judging, our lives are transformed! This can seem an almost impossible task for those who have not experienced the part of themselves that is already a love-finder. But it is the very fact that this part exists within all of us that makes such a transformation not only possible but sometimes surprisingly easy. All that is required is the willingness to closely question every judgment, every unhappy thought—whether directed at ourselves or another—and then to look within for the voice of love. You may be assured that this voice is your gift from your Higher Power, your way to see with love, your honest vision. From a spiritual standpoint, the true purpose of all our relationships is joining, and learning to look from love is simply acknowledging this truth.

It is important to recognize that there is no dishonesty in this approach. You are not being asked to deny "reality" but rather to look from a deeper, more honest, more perceptive reality. And if you will do this, your heart will sing. You will know joy and peace, and you will become a love-finder.

Fourteen
Choosing Peace

Our ego teaches us that the past will predict the future. Because of this we believe that we are constantly in danger of losing everything that is meaningful to us. We think that at any moment we may be attacked, hurt, betrayed, abandoned, and victimized. The eighth principle of Attitudinal Healing reminds us that it is always our own thoughts about the world that cause us distress. It states

We can be peaceful inside regardless of what is happening outside. Despite the chaos in our lives, we can choose to be peaceful, knowing that we are connected and sustained by our loving, peaceful Source.

Our past experiences often make us think that we are helpless and alone. The world looks dangerous, and we feel like fragile little beings who have little or no control over our own lives or the lives of those we love. Is it any wonder that we experience fear and confusion when we contemplate the future? Our ego tells us that such a way of looking is "honest" and "undeniable," and it counsels us to look out for ourselves and to be cynical about the motives of everyone else.

There Is Another Way of Looking

I want you to consider the possibility that the world we see is upside down and that what we think is cause and effect may actually be the opposite. The belief system which we are used to living by teaches that the cause of our distress comes from outside of us. Thus we are always a potential victim of that over which we have no control.

For example, if we want to play tennis and it rains, the weather has ruined our plans and it is "reasonable" for us to be upset. If we are ill and have lost our inner peace, our ego mind will tell us that we lost our peace because of the illness. Therefore, we are helpless before the forces of the world.

Blame Is the Ego's Game

When things go wrong in our lives—whether it's within our relationships, our business, or our health—our "natural" tendency is to find someone to blame. But what happens when we play the ego's destructive game and decide who's to blame? Does that fix anything in our lives? Does that bring back our happiness or our inner peace? Do we feel more loved, more connected? Is our mind made whole? We have all made this mistake, and we have all seen the consequences. Projection and blame destroy our peace, our happiness, and our sense of oneness, and it does nothing for our problems.

In this book I have told many stories about the children who have been my teachers. Unquestionably, all of those children had ample reason to blame the world, and sometimes specific individuals, for their suffering and for what would seem to many to be the loss of their innocence and their very childhoods. If these children can choose not to play the ego's blame game and can return their minds to peace and their lives to joy, surely we too can do the same.

Our Thoughts Create Our Experiences

Perhaps the greatest gift the universe has given us is the freedom to choose what thoughts we put into our minds. This means that every second of every day we can choose peace rather than conflict, regardless of the chaos around us. To minds used to only one way of looking and one response, this can seem an impossible task. But the beautiful truth is that the only choice we are actually making is between happiness and misery. Once we understand that, our desire to consistently choose peace becomes instinctive.

Eulalia and Jack Luckett

For over twenty-two years the Lucketts have been not only our dear friends but also exemplars of the principles of Attitudinal Healing—especially of the eighth principle. Jack, a retired Marine colonel and former assistant district attorney in Los Angeles, was an early executive director of the Center when it was in Tiburon, California. Eulalia was one of the first women to graduate with a Master's in business administration from Harvard.

From lives that had been directed toward achievement and worldly success, they committed themselves to unconditional love and to living without judgments or the need to control events. They gave up most of their possessions and chose to live as simply and as peacefully as they could. To some, this would seem like a sacrifice, and yet Jack and Eulalia are two of the most joyful people we know.

They now have faith in a power greater than themselves that they think of as God. They now know that their happiness and peace come from their connection to God and have nothing to do with the outside world. It's as if they float through life on a river of peace rather than a river of conflict.

This does not mean that they are now exempt from the same challenges we all face. I have seen them deal with illnesses and problems in their relationship as well as the mundane difficulties of everyday life. The difference is that they have accepted the fact that they can choose to deal with their difficulties in peace. They consistently demonstrate the marvelous ability to remain calm, loving, and peaceful, even in the face of chaos.

Each day Jack and Eulalia focus on sharing their unconditional love with everyone they meet. They do this in many ways, one of which is to carry little hearts everywhere they go. In a restaurant, they will ask the waitress what color heart she would like, and often she will pin the heart on her clothes or in her hair, and she will feel this symbol of their love throughout her workday.

All of us have an innocent child inside, and Jack and Eulalia allow theirs to come out and play—something so many adults are afraid or embarrassed to do. They can act in silly ways without being fearful of censure or judgment. And because of their uninhibited joy and exuberance, people are drawn to them and are nourished in their presence.

Our Choice Is Clear

Regardless of our past or present circumstances, we all have the ability to choose to look on ourselves and everyone else with love. Practicing this every day will bring us a joy that cannot be touched by the events of the world.

There is a prayer from *A Course in Miracles* that Diane and I say every day. We think of it as the healer's prayer. It is one of the most powerful prayers I know for getting the ego to step aside so that we can look at the world from the present and remember our connection with our Loving Source. This prayer quiets the chatter of our minds and allows us to become channels of Love as we open our hearts to the voice of Love that resides in all of us:

I am here only to be truly helpful
I am here to represent You who sent me
I do not have to worry about what to say
Or what to do
Because You who sent me will direct me
I am content to be wherever You wish
Knowing You go there with me
*I will be healed as I let You teach me to heal**

Fifteen
All Relationships Are Equal

Most of us are taught that wisdom only comes from years of experience and that the older we are, the more we possess. Many of us also assume that academic degrees and worldly success bestow great wisdom upon those who attain them. At the Center we believe something very different, as the ninth principle of Attitudinal Healing states

> *We are students and teachers to each other.* Peace comes to us when we recognize and demonstrate that all our relationships are equal.

Regardless of age or credentials, everyone at the Center is treated as an equal. We are all teachers and students to each other. When the student is ready, the teacher will appear—and vice versa!

When an individual visits one of our groups at the Center, we ask that all degrees and labels be left outside. We call everyone by their first name, so I am "Jerry" to both adults and children.

For a long time now I have recognized that the children who come to the Center are wise, spiritual beings in young bodies. We have all learned many spiritual truths from them.

The History of the Center

When I was guided to start the Center for Attitudinal Healing, I had an exploratory meeting with nine children who were in various stages of catastrophic illnesses. I shared my thoughts with them and then asked for their ideas. It never occurred to me to see them as less than my equals. I asked for their help, and together we discussed the pros and cons of beginning a group.

Those nine children decided that they would like to meet for six weeks and to determine after that if they wanted to continue. They also made the decision that we should meet on Wednesday evenings from 6:00 to 7:30 P.M. and that they should all get free dinners! After the initial six weeks, the group decided to continue. Later that same year, we also added groups for siblings, parents, and grandparents.

Initially there were three facilitators, who also rotated responsibility for providing meals. After a year of this, I found that I was getting tired of preparing meals and suggested that we begin our meetings a little later in the evening so we could all eat beforehand. I was voted down! Today, twenty-five years later, we still provide free dinners to the children and their families. In fact, all of our direct services at the Center are free. From the beginning it was clear to me that the children felt empowered when they were treated as equals whose opinions were respected and valued. I knew that they had been overloaded with all the "doctor stuff," and I wanted them to know that in all ways we were teachers and students to each other.

We also discovered that the children from our Center who visited schools to talk about their illnesses and what it was like to lose their hair from chemotherapy turned out to be much better consultants than were physicians, psychologists, social workers, or other credentialed adults. After all, they were speaking from life experience, which is the best credential of all.

Eventually we found ourselves being asked to appear on several national television programs, such as *The Phil Donahue Show*, *60 Minutes*, and a special with Fred Rogers. We were also invited onto a number of radio programs. During these times, I purposely stayed in the background, recognizing that these children were powerful teachers of the principles of Attitudinal Healing as they spoke of dealing with pain, shots, and even their fear of death.

In 1986, as part of our "Children as Teachers of Peace" project, Diane and I took seventeen children to China. Three of these children had recovered from cancer, and while there, I was asked to lecture at the Cancer Institute. I agreed to do so as long as they allowed me to bring these three children and to let them speak as well. The evening turned out to be a remarkable, healing experience for everyone involved, and once again, I saw what powerful teachers these children are.

There is also a program to train people who want to volunteer at the Center, to incorporate our approach and philosophy into their own work, or to start other centers. We provide educational outreach through the use of books, articles, audio- and videotapes, and by participating in workshops, giving lectures at medical facilities, and appearing on television and radio shows. There has been a growing interest in our work, and many hospitals are now using our principles. There are now 150 centers in thirty countries.

At our Center in Sausalito we have added groups for those with hepatitis C, for women who have HIV, as well as a general group for those with HIV or AIDS. We also have groups for those with chronic illness and pain and for adults with catastrophic illnesses. We have loss and grief groups for both children and adults.

For some time our Center has reached out to caregivers who often receive little or no support and frequently feel quite alone and overwhelmed. Many elders have to care for a husband or wife with Alzheimer's or other devastating illnesses, and we have begun groups to help these caregivers recognize that they are not alone. We also have a grief and loss group specifically for elders as well.

As part of our community outreach, we have a group for high school kids who wish to learn about Attitudinal Healing. We teach anger management in schools and also have an Attitudinal Healing group at San Quentin Prison.

Another program at the Center is open to everyone, not just to those with catastrophic illnesses or special needs. "Person-to-Person" is for those who wish to incorporate the twelve Attitudinal Healing principles into their lives. The Center serves as the catalytic agent for putting people together who are given the simple instruction that their only aim is to be nonjudgmental, to be love-finders rather than faultfinders, and to practice forgiveness.

In the "Person-to-Person" groups, it is suggested that we work on developing an entirely different kind of mind-set. We resolve beforehand that we will scan the other person for signs of love, gentleness, and peace and that the only information we will retain in our mind is that which will permit us to continue looking upon this person kindly. In other words, we seek only their innocence, not their guilt. We look at them from our heart, not from our preconceived notions.

I am frequently asked how we manage financially, since all of our direct services are free. When I received the inner guidance to start the Center, I also heard, "Don't worry about money; just do the work and what money you need will be provided. Trust in God." The guidance also stated that I was to volunteer my own time, which I am still doing. For years, the staff consisted mainly of unpaid volunteers. As the Center expanded, we have added some paid positions but still rely heavily on the many volunteers who so generously contribute their time.

For the first two years, I paid the rent, phone bills, and other overhead. Then a dear friend and benefactor, John Robinson, began to give us monthly financial support. As we became better known, we began to receive many contributions, from very small to larger ones. Later, we were awarded several large grants from foundations.

We Can Only Help an Equal

Group meetings start and end with everyone closing their eyes, joining hands, and experiencing our oneness and unity. We share problems, inspirations, experiences, as well as practical ideas that we have found to be helpful, and as we do this we practice seeing each other as a teacher. The emphasis is on equality, regardless of age or background. This means the facilitators also talk about their problems.

To aid us we sometimes use meditation, relaxation techniques, positive active imagination (mental imagery), art, and prayer. We help each other with specific problems such as

- I'm embarrassed to go to school because I lost all my hair after chemotherapy.

- I'm lonely and scared when I'm in the hospital.

- Why did this happen to me?

- I'm jealous of my brother because he gets all the attention because he's sick.

- I'm afraid that my child is going to die.

- My wife is withdrawing from me because I'm sick. I hate her for this and yet I love her and don't want to lose her.

- I just found out I'm HIV-positive, and my parents don't even know I'm gay.

- I love my husband, but I'm feeling overwhelmed trying to care for him, as if my life is draining away.

We offer strength and support to each other by sharing similar problems and how we might handle them but most of all by listening in a completely nonjudgmental, defenseless way and by extending unconditional love and acceptance.

Some years ago I visited a hospice in New Zealand where I met a volunteer who had her name on the pin she was wearing, and just beneath the pin was the word *Listener*. This told me everything about her. She was not there to give advice, to fix anyone, or to prescribe some course of action. Listening *is* loving. Loving *is* listening. Listening does require attention but not necessarily action, and it may be the most important and meaningful thing we can do for someone who is dying. Because we know this is true, our Centers pay a lot of attention to learning how to listen and how to be completely present for another person.

Charlene Sugawara

Through the years I have been repeatedly reminded that, regardless of how old we are, we always teach what we need to learn, and as we teach, we are able to incorporate the principles of Attitudinal Healing more firmly into our lives. We recently received this letter from Charlene, who came to the Center as a child:

> *Dear Jerry and Diane,*
>
> *It's been a long time since you've seen or heard from me . . . I know that your schedule is busy, but I thought you would like to know that I am still around.*
>
> *It was almost twenty years ago. . . .*
>
> *I remember walking into Jerry's office in Tiburon with my parents, very scared, feeling very alone. I was very sick, my doctors didn't have much hope, and even at eight I knew something was wrong. My doctor recommended trying this new group he had heard was located in Tiburon, and my parents decided to try it out.*
>
> *I remember walking into a group session, very nervous, but also shocked to see that there were other children, various ages, but in the same situation. I didn't participate much at first, but I soon became at ease with the Center and its activities.*
>
> *My mother and I went with Jerry on one of his trips to Hawaii in 1980, and I went with the two of you on a fantastic trip to China in 1986. The qualities of love, inner strength, and peace have been instilled into my heart, and more important, into my soul.*
>
> *Today, despite the odds, the medical records, how sick my body was, I am still here. I have graduated from both high school and college and have had a full time job at Pacific Bell for almost five years. I own a condo very close to my parents.*
>
> *I believe that the lessons I started to learn at the Center have brought me where I am today. I am very happy with the person I have become; glad that I have taken on good traits from my parents and those around me.*

I believe that God has let me survive for a reason, to help those who are where I once was years ago. I have tried to share my beliefs with others who are in need, especially those who have friends or relatives with cancer.

I let them know that they can't let anyone tell them whether or not they will live, or how long they have left, for that is just letting someone else put limits on what you are able to do. Just let life come as it will, to not worry about the negative things, but believe the positive, for if you truly believe it, it will happen. After all, I am living proof.

With God's eternal love and comforting peace.

Diane and I read Charlene's letter with tears of joy in our eyes. Here was a powerful witness to the lasting value of Attitudinal Healing and to the truth that we are all teachers and students to each other. Occasionally I meet someone who expresses the thought that what we did in establishing the Center was a great gift to the children who come there, and sometimes there is even the unspoken impression that perhaps our work involves a sacrifice of some kind. I have to smile at that because those of us who have been intimately involved with the Center know that it is we who have been blessed.

Indeed, it is impossible to work with the children who come to the Center without recognizing the sacredness, holiness, and innocence of their hearts. I often think that the essence of our work is bringing to life the biblical passage, "And a little child shall lead them." I now know that children are the best teachers of unconditional love. They also teach us honesty, because they cannot have a real relationship with us if there is deception. When you treat children as equals and are willing to learn from them, you begin to experience a reflection of their innocence in your own heart.

Bobby

Early in the history of the Center, I made a "house call" on a fourteen-year-old boy named Bobby, who was dying of cancer. None of the drugs that were then available were able to stop the progression of his disease. When I first met him, he looked gray and ashen and could barely speak. He was receiving morphine by an intravenous drip for his pain.

As I was sitting beside this gravely ill boy, I felt guided to ask him for a favor. I knew that I had a tape recorder in my briefcase, and I told Bobby that neither I nor any of the other volunteers at the Center had ever been with a fourteen-year-old who was facing death. I told him that I knew he could be of immense help to other children who would soon be facing what he was now going through and asked him if he would be willing to talk into the recorder. He agreed to do so, and as soon as he began speaking, his grayness and pallor began to disappear and his eyes became brighter. As he talked he became more energetic and eventually was able to sit up in bed.

What I had done was to allow Bobby to enter into the consciousness of helping and giving to others. As I have mentioned previously, whenever we focus on giving to others with love, we take our attention away from our bodies. This has been an important lesson for the children and adults at the Center who are dealing with illness, pain, and the possibility of death. But it has been of equal importance to those of us who have seen what a powerful lesson this is and how we can transform our own lives through consciously expressing love.

Bobby died a few weeks after my visit, but his voice and his gift of love live on in a tape that continues to help others.

Mother Teresa once told Diane and me about a woman in Argentina who had impressed her so much by naming her newborn son "Professor of Love." No matter what age her child was, this mother couldn't help but remember that he was there as a teacher of love. We all need such reminders, because the essence of Attitudinal Healing is learning to be a teacher of love.

$\mathcal{S}ixteen$
Becoming Whole

When the world is viewed from the separate "little self," it is perceived and responded to as a series of disconnected parts. Such a picture must always appear chaotic and confusing, and can only reinforce a sense of powerlessness, isolation, and division. The tenth principle of Attitudinal Healing recognizes the importance of a healed vision. It states

We can focus on the whole of our lives rather than on the fragments. It is an illusion to believe that our lives are separate from each other. Healing is focusing on our interconnectedness with each other and all living things.

When we look at the world with the eyes of our ego, it's like peering through a kaleidoscope and seeing all these tiny fragments but never the whole. Viewed this way, our life makes no sense, and we shift with every twist and turn and never find our center. When we stop looking through the lens of the ego, we gain a different perspective that allows us to make new choices. In truth, we are all part of an interwoven fabric that encompasses all of life and blankets the world with oneness. We simply are not separate from each other. For many of us, the experience of oneness and unity has been so brief and tenuous that it is hardly given credence except as an idealistic but impractical concept. But how will it ever be believed if we continue to focus on separation? Like scientists who spend their lives looking through the lens of a high-powered microscope and see only tiny segments but make all sorts of pronouncements about the whole, we think we are seeing accurately. But we are not.

A Museum

Have you ever been to a museum and stood very close to a large work of art? If so, perhaps you noticed that you were not only unable to make out the theme of the painting but often could see only blotches of formless color. As you moved further away from the painting, you began to make out certain objects—perhaps a face and a hand. As you continued to move back until you could see the entire painting clearly, the theme was obvious.

We too must achieve "distance" in order to see the whole. Rather than literally moving back, we must symbolically take our eyes off of fragments and figuratively step back until we are able to see the whole. Obviously this is a mental process that requires us to look without judgment and to be willing to see from the present rather than the past.

Most of us have had the experience of meeting an individual who has been described to us as "angry" or "not very attractive" and being surprised because this is not our experience of this person. It is as if we are meeting an entirely different individual—as indeed we are.

What has been described to us is only a perception, and perceptions are personal and colored by our judgments and opinions. Once we realize this, we can choose to see people more broadly and lovingly. Egos often become stuck and view everything from the perspective of the high-powered microscope.

When we look this way, it's easy to magnify faults and differences. We notice a small, negative thing about another person and unless we choose to look more broadly—to power-down that microscope—soon the fault becomes all that we can see.

One way of seeing more broadly is to imagine we are standing on top of a mountain, looking down. Everything below seems small and insignificant. It's impossible to pick out and obsess about some little detail. Indeed, we may wonder why we allow our egos to make such a fuss about things that are so meaningless.

Mountains

We think of climbing mountains both symbolically and literally. Mountains often represent overcoming difficulties and achieving goals. And we recognize that standing on top of a mountain provides us with an exceptional view because we can look down and see how everything is interconnected. Most of us have also had the experience of flying over a city or town and looking down at what appears to be a well-ordered, perfect little society.

Many of the astronauts who have viewed earth from space had a similar experience, and many of them expressed this in spiritual terms. They no longer saw the separation. They saw the whole. They no longer saw disconnected, warring countries with separate, warring interests. They saw a beautiful blue sphere that was perfectly placed and perfectly harmonious.

Who is to say that unity is an illusion simply because we are used to looking at fragments? Perhaps if we were to assume a vision of wholeness, we would indeed see wholeness.

Another common experience that many of us have had is losing all sense of time, space, and even our bodies as we sat at a concert listening to beautiful music. We felt as if we were a part of the music, the musicians, and the people around us. Perhaps it is time to recognize and accept that these experiences of connection are as valid as, and I would say, far more valid than, our experiences of separation.

"Me First" Relationships

Most of us think that we are lacking something and so we look for a partner to complete us—someone to fill in the holes that we believe our past has created. Or perhaps we are simply critical of ourselves for being, say, shy and so we look for someone outgoing to fix us. Our partner probably has similar needs and is looking to us for completion as well.

Obviously both people long to be made whole, but relationships that are formed from the neediness of each individual will always be fractured because we cannot complete ourselves by getting a "missing piece" from someone else. We are not jigsaw puzzles that need to be put together by another person. But as long as we think of ourselves in this way, we will look outside for completion, and we will be disappointed. We will continue seeing ourselves and each other as fragmented. Indeed, if our relationship fails, we often have the sense that our ex-partner absconded with a few of our pieces.

Even though these "me first" relationships can feel like love, they are more of a trade arrangement or bargain between two separate selves who cannot see wholeness anywhere they look.

Bodies and Body Parts

We tend to live our lives in segments, and we experience our bodies in the same way. If the gym is our focus, we may think of ourselves as our muscles, and when we look at other bodies, we compare our muscles to theirs. If we are overweight, we see ourselves as our fat, and we usually launch into a battle against our own body. If a woman centers on her breasts and becomes preoccupied with that aspect of herself and other women, she may even rate herself by how the men in her life react to her breasts.

It is tempting for those who have cancer to think of that aspect of their lives as who they are. When I was a child, I defined myself by my reading problem. And, of course, most of us define ourselves by our jobs: teacher, lawyer, carpenter, artist, plumber, and so on. And we relate to each other in the same way. If you find out that a close friend has cancer, you will often relate to her as a "cancer victim."

This fractured way of experiencing ourselves and others is so habitual that it seems accurate. But what we don't look at is the effect this separation has on ourselves and others. What happens when we are no longer able to define ourselves by our profession or our appearance or that which makes us "special"?

One of the universal responses people who visit our Center have is how "healthy" and "normal" the children seem. Because they expect to meet children who are victims of their diseases, they are amazed when the children they meet are happy and peaceful. But when we make a consistent effort to "step back" and see each other's wholeness rather than what sets us apart, we begin to experience our own wholeness as well.

Co-joined Twin Imagery

Using our imaginations allows us to bypass our separate, fragmented selves. One imagery that is particularly helpful is to actively think of everyone we meet as our spiritual co-joined twin. If we truly do this consistently, we will not want to judge or attack anyone, because we recognize that we would be attacking ourselves as well. Children rarely have difficulty using their imaginations in this way, but adults often feel that such imageries are beneath them or are unsophisticated. But if you will suspend this cynical fragment of yourself for just one day, the experience of oneness, peace, and happiness that you will have will convince you that in reality our minds are already joined and that what you are now seeing is simply the truth which was always there.

How Far Does Love Go?

Once we believe that the world is whole and that we are a complete part of that whole, we can then believe that sending love and receiving love have no boundaries. Distance is no barrier, and it is not necessary for us to be physically present with the object of our love. And because love cannot be contained, it spreads throughout the world of oneness and blesses all who recognize wholeness.

The healed mind, the undivided mind, sends forth blessings that are like pebbles of love dropped into a lake, creating ripples of love that travel farther than our eyes can see and affect every part of the lake. Unquestionably, love has a ripple effect. It expands upon itself and has no limitations.

Recent scientific studies have recognized the power of prayer and meditation on those who are ill and live miles away from the one who is praying. At the Center we have all experienced this connection on a very deep level, and we are now convinced that minds are truly joined and that the recognition of this truth allows us to offer healing to ourselves and others.

Whole Relationships

We all long for relationships that reflect oneness, because we recognize that it is in seeing each other as whole that we heal our minds and experience unity. But it requires daily effort to free ourselves from our old way of seeing only a world of fragments.

Two people who come together with the recognition that they are complete spiritual beings who are only temporarily inhabiting bodies are able to experience the abundance of love and peace that their Creator has given them. They do not see a fragmented world but a world of Love in which all life is connected. They experience themselves as part of everything and everyone, and they know that there is no separation between themselves and that which created them.

Such a relationship is "we" oriented. Two souls come together as one; two lights unite and become a more brilliant source of illumination; two hearts beat as one. Such a union is the most powerful healing force in the world because it gently answers the question of who we really are.

Beyond Separation

It has always fascinated me that when we learn to consciously help and give to others, we lose awareness of our separate identities. True love is changeless and eternal. It is an expanding energy that endlessly unfolds and blesses all that it touches and brings healing and wholeness to minds that are shattered and fearful. When we look beyond the body and choose to see the light of Love in another person, we are seeing who that person truly is. And in their reflection, we see ourselves completely whole and abundantly blessed by the reality of Love.

Seventeen
There Is Another Reality

Our old way of thinking causes us to view life fearfully and to see death as the end of our reality. We think of ourselves and those we love as bodies, and we know that bodies are fragile and vulnerable. From this perspective, it is logical to go through life in fear and to dread death. But there is another reality, and the eleventh principle of Attitudinal Healing acknowledges this. It states

> *Because love is eternal, death need not be viewed as fearful.*
> We begin to let go of our fear of death when we truly believe that what is real never changes and that Love is always present.

A reality based on the physical senses can acknowledge only the story that the body tells. And of course this is a story with an unhappy ending. But there is another tale—a tale of Love that is eternal, a story of another reality that is changeless and timeless. This is the story our lives tell once we believe that we are more than a body and that our true identity lies outside of what changes, gets sick, suffers, and dies.

Once we accept Love as our true identity and recognize that Love and life are one, we let go of not only our fear of death but also our fear of the future. The body simply is not our reality, and this truth frees us to live with boundless hope, peace, and unity. We are one with our Higher Power, and our lives begin to demonstrate the ancient truth that "perfect love casts out fear."

Other Forms of Death

We often experience death in ways that are not related to the body. Divorce can feel like the death of a marriage, and one or both partners may suffer tremendous grief and pain. Losing a job can be experienced as the loss of one's identity and meaning. Even the natural function of aging is often borne as a kind of curse that deprives us of our youth and vitality. These are all challenges carrying emotional charges that can leave us feeling drained and depressed. It is our willingness to face these emotions and the beliefs behind them which is crucial in remembering that we are more than the stories our bodies tell.

Being Half-Dead

Although we may be physically well, many of us go through the day feeling half-dead because of all the judgments we make. To the ego, our primary function in life is judging and interpreting the behavior of other bodies to see who is guilty and who is innocent. But we cannot do this without feeling disconnected and empty, which leads to the greatest malady of all—spiritual deprivation. In the shadow of this half-life, our daily activities often seem meaningless. We become afraid of life, of love and intimacy, of joy and happiness; we frequently find that we can commit to nothing, not even ourselves. In this deadened state we are numb to the beauty and mystery of life.

As I look back over my own life, I now see that for too many years I walked around half-dead. I was depressed and agitated at the same time. In spite of a successful professional life, I felt something missing in my heart. I now know that what I was experiencing was an emptiness of Spirit. I was so plugged into getting and judging that my spiritual gas tank was constantly empty.

Without being consciously aware of it, much of my time was spent in fear and in making judgments about others and about myself. It is extremely difficult, if not impossible, to experience the Spirit within when one is locked into such an unhappy and lonely approach to life.

I have witnessed many people die whose spirit grew stronger even as their bodies deteriorated from disease. I have seen those who embraced life to their last breath because they understood that the death of the body was not the end of their being. In many ways they were more "alive" than those of us who walk through life with empty souls and with minds focused on guilt and separation.

Our spirits long to soar like eagles, to be filled with inspiration, to feel the love that flows between us and our Creator. But until we are willing to relinquish all forms of judgment and attack, we will remain half-dead and unaware of the splendor that awaits us.

Manifestations of Fear

I once had a patient whose morning ritual was to open his newspaper to the obituary section. When I asked him about this, he explained that he just wanted to check to see if any of his friends had died. On further exploration, I discovered that in a strange way reading the obituaries reassured him that he was still alive! After all, his name was not listed!

Behavior such as this might seem strange or even crazy, but this gentleman had a tremendous fear of death, and to him the behavior was logical and helped alleviate some of his fear—at least for that day.

Most of us acknowledge that making a will is a wise and loving thing to do, a gift to those we leave behind. Why then do so many of us put it off? The answer is simple. Making a will requires us to directly confront the fact that we are going to die, and so we think of hundreds of reasons why we can't do it now.

Fear of Death

Our ego works overtime creating all kinds of fear for us to worry about. It is my impression that one of our biggest fears, whether we are conscious of it or not, is the fear of death. And I am also convinced that buried beneath this fear is our fear of God.

We all have our individual ways of avoiding the issue of death and dying. Some of us become workaholics and fill our days and nights with an endless array of activities that keep our fears at bay—at least for a while. Although we may have the appearance of one who is successful and accomplished, we may also be numb to our emotions and feelings.

Often we try to control our fear of death by controlling the events and people in our lives, as if the ability to manage every situation will magically allow us to control our destiny as well.

Yours Truly

It's a little embarrassing for me to share the thoughts I used to have about death and dying, but I want you to understand that for the first fifty years of my life, I was terrified of death. So was my father. I remember that as we were leaving his sister's funeral, he found a hose outside the funeral parlor and stopped to wash his hands. I was shocked by his behavior and asked him what he was doing. He replied, "It's an old-world superstition that when you go to a funeral you should wash your hands so you won't be the next one to die." He was so fearful that he couldn't wait to get home to protect himself!

When I thought of myself as an atheist, I became even more fearful of dying. After my marriage of twenty years ended in 1973, I turned to alcohol to numb my guilt and pain. My mind was so fractured that even as I was drinking myself to death, I remained terrified of dying.

We've all heard about the companies that will "freeze" your body at death so that if a new drug—or even the magical fountain of youth—is discovered, you can be "thawed out," fixed up, and resume your life. At the time I first read about such a procedure, my fear of death was so extreme that I remember being comforted by the thought. Although I didn't do anything about it, it seemed like such a good idea!

Letting Go of Our Fear of Death

I will forever be grateful to the seven-year-old boy who, during morning rounds at the University of California Medical Center, asked the oncologist, "What is it like to die?" The oncologist quickly changed the subject, and I recognized that perhaps he was too fearful to handle such a deep and meaningful question, a question that is on the minds of almost everyone at one time or another. It was certainly a question that I was wrestling with. I later discovered that many children at this hospital were having honest and fearless conversations about death with people like the cleaning woman who was mopping their floor and was not encumbered by academic degrees or beliefs about what children should or should not talk about.

The Center for Attitudinal Healing was founded in part because of this little boy's question, but by that time my life and belief system had changed dramatically. I often say that the Center was established for people like me who were willing to learn from children facing life-threatening illnesses that there is another way of looking at death and at life.

At the Center in Sausalito, our Level One workshops in Attitudinal Healing always include a powerful experiential exercise in death. We divide the workshop into groups of ten and ask each group to decide who will be the dying patient and who will be the mother, father, daughter, son, friend, and so on. We ask each group to use their imaginations in a way that will make the experience quite real. The fact that we go through boxes of tissues during this process shows that most who come are successful in getting in touch with their feelings and expressing them.

Each member of the group begins to see where their particular fears about death are centered. In one session, a fifty-year-old man volunteered to be the son and later told us that his mother, with whom he had an unhealed relationship, was dying in another city. He shared the angry feelings that he still had from the past, but by the end of the workshop, he expressed the belief that his relationship with his mother would never be the same. The experience had allowed him to recognize the importance of forgiveness and to work on releasing his anger.

During another workshop, a woman who had recently been diagnosed with cancer volunteered to be the dying patient. She stated that her group experience had allowed her to get in touch with feelings which she had been unaware of. She had been able to process them, and now her fear of dying seemed to have vanished.

It is always important to fully acknowledge and honor our humanness and our human feelings, for as you can see, this allows us to begin to recognize a greater reality. This is why it is equally important that we not enshrine our human feelings and become attached to them as if they represent all that we are.

Attitudinal Healing acknowledges the truth of our shared identity—an identity that is not contained in the body, an identity that is changeless and eternal, an identity that does not fear death, because it receives its purpose and its meaning from Love.

Beyond the Body

One of our many teachers was a girl named Jennifer, who had been on dialysis for years because of a kidney abnormality. She became very close to Diane and began to incorporate the principles of Attitudinal Healing into her life. Because of her illness, she was forced to spend a tremendous amount of time in hospitals, where she discovered that one of the things she liked best was helping other kids with their fears.

Shortly before she died, Jennifer was on a television program with other people who had serious illnesses. Each of them was asked this question: "If you knew that you had only one week to live, how would you want to spend those days?"

When it was Jennifer's turn to speak, she stated that she would call or write everyone with whom she had an unhealed relationship and forgive them. She went on to add that she would rather go through life with a sickness and help others than to be healthy but self-centered.

We See What We Believe

Having spent the last twenty-five years working with and learning from children and adults who were facing the possibility of dying, I now believe with all my heart and soul that there is no death, because our true identity is not limited to a body. To me, bodies are only the transient houses of our souls, which are eternal and never die. Every morning, Diane and I say this prayer from *A Course in Miracles* because it reminds us of our real identity:

I am not a body
I am free
For I am still
As God created me

I want the Peace of God
The Peace of God is everything that I want
The aim of all my living here
The end that I seek
My purpose, my function and my life
*While I abide where I am not at home.**

To believe in death, we must accept our bodies as our only reality. When we remind ourselves daily that our identity is not a body and that our only goal is the Peace of God, we open our hearts to the truth of who we are and the Light of God pours into every fiber of our being.

If you want to let go of your attachment to your body, you might try looking beyond your senses by imagining that there is a love filter over your eyes and ears so you see and hear only Love. When we become faultfinders, we immediately feel separate and identify with our body, which is the source of our fear. As love-finders we identify with our spiritual self and experience our connection with that which is eternal.

I Am the Light

Something unique happens when we wake in the morning and remind ourselves that we are the Light of the World. When we truly believe that our purpose here is to shine that Light and to see only that Light in others, we begin to experience joy, peace, and happiness. But if we are to experience Oneness with each other and with that which created us, it is essential that we continue to look beyond the body and the costumes which people wear. As we practice this happy lesson, our fear of death begins to dissipate until it is just a distant memory of another time.

Is There a Prescription for Dying?

I do not believe that there is a prescription for how to die. Unfortunately, many of us have a formula or script about how we think another person should go through the dying process. Many of us want to see the dying person as peaceful and without pain during their last days. Some of us believe that we should try to get the one who is dying to turn to God, or we may have a specific plan that we want them to follow.

At the Center we believe that it is extremely important not to have any script for a dying person. We have learned that our absolute acceptance of where this person is now is the most important gift we can give. I also know that what we say is not nearly as important as our willingness to listen without judgment and to be completely present.

When I am with a dying person, I go within to the Source that connects us to learn what I should say or do. More often than not the message I hear is "simply to be and do nothing." This usually means that I am to be comfortable in the silence or perhaps to gently hold the person's hand and extend a silent blessing of love and acceptance.

At other times I may be instructed to open the door to possible issues the person may have regarding forgiveness. There is no question that the forgiveness process may be of extreme importance for many people facing death—for themselves, their family, and others who may be involved. On the other hand, the person may simply not be ready or interested in any discussions along this line. I believe that it is extremely important for us to open doors for each other, but we must never push or pull another through that door. Always it must come from them and be a completely free choice.

Being Present

If there is one thing I have learned from the many teachers at the Center, it is the importance of extending unconditional love in the present, whether that means being comfortable in silence or simply helping in whatever way I can. I have also learned that my own inner peace and lack of fear are crucial in extending love and acceptance.

Having so many people allow me to step into the intimacy of their hearts has been a sacred and holy gift that I treasure. I awaken each morning feeling so fortunate to be allowed to do the work that I do. To be able to give and receive love is a blessing that is beyond words.

Eighteen
Answering with Love

Once we experience our connection with others, we will want to choose to respond from peace in all of our encounters. The twelfth and last principle of Attitudinal Healing states

> *We can always see ourselves and others as either extending love or giving a call for help.* Rather than seeing anger and attack, it is always possible for us to recognize a call for help and to answer with love.

When we choose to change our perception of others and to see them as either loving or sending us a fearful call for help, we then have the choice to respond from our connection and our love. This frees us to feel the presence of peace.

However, if we continue to believe that "attack" comes from outside, we will always find a way of defending ourselves and attacking back. Rather than perceiving others as attacking, we can learn to see them as fearful and asking for love. This way of looking takes practice and discipline, but it can be accomplished. Dropping out of the "attack/defend/attack" game allows us to touch a very beautiful place in our heart—the place that knows the truth and responds from love.

By reminding ourselves that there are only two emotions—love and fear—life becomes less complex. When we see someone who is acting from anger and judgment, we can recognize that they are fearful and need our love and support. No one who is angry and upset has ever been helped by more anger and attack. Love is truly the great healing force in the world.

Lessons in Iran

I like telling this story because it illustrates so perfectly the difference between choosing fear and choosing love. In 1996, Diane and I were invited to lecture in Iran. Five of our books had been published there, and we were to speak at the Cancer Institute. Because there is no United States embassy in Iran, many of our friends tried to persuade us not to go, expressing the fear that if we happened to say the wrong thing, we could easily be thrown in prison.

Despite these well-meant warnings, our guidance was to go and to choose to be peaceful rather than fearful. When we got to our hotel, we were greeted by a large banner at the entrance that read "Down with Americans." The desk clerk, however, was extremely friendly and said we were the first Americans to stay there in several years.

When we arrived at the lecture hall the following day, the auditorium was full. We were to give our talk in English, but just before we began speaking, our interpreter pointed to a tall man in a black turban and said that he was there from the government to make sure that we didn't "say anything wrong."

After we had been speaking for a while, I could feel that everyone was enjoying the talk. Then I happened to notice that "the man from the government" looked angry and was frowningly taking notes. All my concepts about Attitudinal Healing went right out the window, and I became fearful, wondering if Diane and I were going to wind up in jail. It was my impression that Diane was experiencing the same emotions.

After a few minutes of letting my fears run rampant, I remembered the twelfth principle and chose to think of this man as fearful and sending out a call for help. Silently I began to send him love, but I was not attached to making his behavior change, and it did not. However, I began to feel much more peaceful.

When we finished our talk, the director of the Institute gave a ten-minute summary in Farsi, which is the national language of Iran. As he finished, many people began to come up to shake hands and tell us how much they had enjoyed the talk. All of a sudden, "the man from the government" was standing right in front of us. And he had his own interpreter. He began apologizing and said that he could not understand a single word of English and had been frustrated throughout our talk but wanted to let us know how much he had enjoyed the Farsi translation because he agreed with everything we were saying. He added that he hoped our message would reach many people in Iran. What I had seen as anger and the possibility of attack was simply a projection of my own fears!

We gave several other lectures in Iran and consistently found the people there to be friendly and helpful. For me, the experience was a powerful demonstration of the twelfth principle.

A Lesson from Peru

Several years ago while we were lecturing in Peru, Diane and I took a couple of days off to go hiking in the Andes Mountains. I wanted to find a shaman. This desire came to me from my eldest brother, Les, who is now deceased but who had spent considerable time in Peru.

Les was a biochemist who had gone to places in Peru that most Americans had never seen. He would go to obscure villages and ask the shaman for the plants that they were using to cure various illnesses, particularly mental illness and cancer, and he would bring these plants back to the States to study.

Rather high in the mountains, we found a shaman who was the healer for his village. Through an interpreter I asked him how they treated mental illness. To my absolute surprise, he stated that it was their belief that people who suffer from mental illness are suffering from fear and lack of love, and so they simply love them.

I asked another question: "What happens to mentally ill patients who are so angry that they attack others and are destructive? Do you send them down to the city to be hospitalized?"

Again, his response stunned me. He replied, "No, we do not ever send our people to the hospital for the mentally ill. We believe that those mentally ill people who are angry and destructive are suffering from a deeper lack of love. Our treatment for them is to give even more love."

Having expected to find something completely different, I discovered that high in the Andes people were practicing Attitudinal Healing and demonstrating the twelfth principle in a very deep way.

Nineteen
The Example of Love

The Aberi family differed from the other families at the Center in several ways. A boy was born to the mother, Mary, after it was discovered she had cancer. The grandparents were actively involved with the Center as well, so we were relating to three generations. Of all the families I have worked with, perhaps none has given me such an in-depth experience with the various stages of life. They taught me a new perspective on birth and death as well as on parenting and grandparenting. The opportunity to become part of this extended family was one of the most meaningful experiences of my life.

Mary Aberi was a person whose life exemplified everything I have said in this book. Her love extended, and is still extending, to many people.

Mary was referred to me by her physician when she was thirty years old. At the time of our meeting, her son, Matty, was one and a half and was sunlight personified. Her husband, George, a manager at IBM, was handsome, sensitive, and full of love.

She and George had waited eight years before she conceived, and her pregnancy was a cause for much celebration. During the early months, her natural beauty and vitality became even more accentuated. Then, in the sixth month, cancer of the breast was diagnosed, and in the seventh, a mastectomy was performed. A bone scan was negative and the prognosis was optimistic.

Matty, a very healthy baby, was delivered by cesarean section. He was so beautiful and radiant that some of their friends called him "the Christ child." Part of Mary's heart was exuberant with joy, but another part was frightened that she might not live long enough to see her son grow up and witness the fruition of all the things she dreamed for him.

Until Matty was about six months of age, Mary seemed to be doing quite well, but then the cancer spread to her bones. Chemotherapy was started and she lost her hair. She began to experience pain, and medication did not seem to help. There was now great apprehension among the family members, and it was at this time that she we referred to me.

On our first meeting, I felt drawn into Mary's light. She was spiritually luminescent, and I knew immediately that she was going to be a significant teacher to me. Feelings of inner beauty, peace, and unconditional love just seemed to radiate from her. I can't adequately describe the experience.

Initially, we met in my office twice a week, and she attended the Center's Tuesday-night adult healing group. As time went on and her physical condition worsened, I saw her almost daily at home, and when I didn't see her we talked on the phone. I learned that as a young adult she had strayed from her religion and because of the seeming unfairness of her current problems was now having some mental battles with God. We became close spiritual partners and psychotherapists to each other. Mary would tell me her problems and I would tell her mine. Later, a great deal of our time together was spent praying. We became witnesses to the Light of God in each other even when we were having trouble seeing it in ourselves. And the rest of the Aberi family took me in as well. I often joined them for meals, played with Matty, and loved and received love from George and from Matty's grandparents.

Patsy Robinson, Carleta Schwartz, Jonelle Simpson, and many others from our "Person-to-Person" program visited Mary regularly. Each in her own way commented that she came away having received more than she had given. No one could really articulate what happened in her presence, but I do know that we all experienced the Peace of God.

Mary became active in our telephone network. She gave courage, hope, and love in abundance and helped others deal with their pain while also learning to use Attitudinal Healing to lessen her own discomfort. There was a quality in her voice that filled the listener with peace, even over the phone.

During this period, Shari Podersky, a young woman from Vancouver, came to see me because of a brain tumor she had developed, and I suggested she visit Mary. When she came back, she said that she was so high she didn't need a plane to fly home. Later, Shari also began to give help over the phone. The linkage she experienced with Mary unfolded like a circle of love, always extending and expanding.

I remember one evening in the hospital when Mary was receiving large doses of morphine every four hours for the severe pain. I found her sleeping when I arrived, so I just held her hand in silence and prayed. Suddenly, the phone rang. The operator said it was an emergency call for me. It was a man in Wyoming with cancer of the lung who was in pain and asking for help. The phone had awakened Mary and she heard my conversation. She asked to talk to him. As she shared her love and gave him some simple imageries to use, I saw the blood rushing back into her cheeks, and for that moment, she was the picture of health.

Six months later when she was hospitalized again, she had a roommate, a woman who was dying of cancer and probably had no more than a few days to live. When I arrived, Mary asked me to talk with the woman and her family. I forgot what

I said, but I do remember what they said. They told me that they felt Mary was truly an angel and that just being and talking with her had helped them let go of their fear and despair.

Possibly more than anyone I have known, Mary chose not to identify with her body. Instead, she believed in spiritual reality as her true being and understood the importance of living in the present. Thus, she conveyed a sense of peace to everyone around her. In giving peace, she was able to experience it herself. She was a living demonstration of the principle that to give is to receive.

Of the many things Mary and I taught each other, the most significant was that words are not necessary. The best moments we spent together were the silent ones, with joined hands and in prayer, giving gratitude for being in God's presence and feeling the infinity of God's peace and love. As her trust in God increased, her peace radiated, and her family began to feel their fears dissipate.

One night, I left Mary's house about 10:30 P.M. Although she was weak, she could talk and was very peaceful. About 2 A.M., I received a call from George, her husband, who said that she had gone into a coma. I went back to the house immediately. The whole family was there. I knew what God and Mary wanted me to do. I was to share my own peace with everyone, to see her light, and to not identify with her body. I knew that she had waited so I could be there to help her family through this transition. Mary died at 4 A.M.

One week later, we had a celebration of life at our Center in honor of Mary. Jeanne Carter, a staff member, said, "I used to go up and see Mary at lunchtime when I was having a difficult day, and she had a remarkable ability to see right to the center of a situation, to get rid of all the garbage and junk, and in such a gentle and loving manner, to help me see that everything was really OK. I would always come back feeling very happy, very light, and full of joy. She had a remarkable gift for clearing away all the nonessentials, and when you got down to the core of the problem, there was nothing there. She was a beautiful person.

"One day my daughter, Janet, was visiting, and Mary wanted to meet her. She wasn't really receiving new people, but she wanted to meet Janet, so I drove her over and we went in. Mary was losing her hair again, was swollen, and if you just looked at the body, I guess she wasn't very pretty, but her radiance was beautiful. When we left, I resisted the temptation to ask my daughter what she thought of Mary because everybody thought so much of her, but Janet said spontaneously, 'She is the most beautiful woman I have ever seen.' That was all you saw of Mary—her beauty."

Another staff member, Patsy Robinson, in reference to Shari Podersky's visit with Mary, had this to say: "So Mary sat there and talked to this woman, and I just listened. It was as if God was speaking through Mary. She was saying the most beautiful things to Shari, and there was a—we use the word *transformation*, and maybe we use it too lightly—but I saw it with my eyes; I saw this woman transformed from such a fearful state into a peaceful state. And Mary's peace was extending to me also. And Shari's mother and father were sitting on a piano bench listening, and suddenly her father leaned over and touched me. Mary was engrossed at this point, talking to Shari. He had tears in his eyes as he said, "I don't believe this is happening."

Shari expressed her feelings this way: "Well, my first introduction to Mary was quite by surprise. Patsy said there was this wonderful, marvelous person that I'd have to meet, and she phoned Mary, who said we could come up. My mom and dad and I went to see her.

We walked in and she greeted us. Her little boy was asleep in the playpen. I walked into her room, and it was completely peaceful. And for me—I get very emotional talking about it—it was the first time that I was ever in a really peaceful place. I wasn't very peaceful myself at that time. Then she sat down and just started talking and teaching. She glowed all the time. I think it was the most moving experience I ever had. I don't know what else to tell you. I think that she is beautiful."

That day, we phoned John in Wyoming. John was the emergency caller Mary talked with the night I was in her room at the hospital. About Mary, he said: "From Mary I learned that everything has its purpose, although we may not understand it. That everything is OK. I often called her when I was really down, and she had a way of responding which would help me see that the universe is in order and that the things which were happening to both of us were not tragic. Sometimes we even talked about funerals and, not trying to be silly or anything, we'd end up laughing about the whole concept of dying and how important it was for us to have a nice funeral—without being morbid, you know.

"The first conversation I had with her in the room there, we seemed to click—I don't know whether psychically or spiritually—and it was as if two old friends who hadn't seen one another in a long time had just been reunited. As our relationship developed, we seemed to call one another at times when both of us needed to talk and had been thinking of each other. Mary had a way of saying, 'John, you're my teacher. I learn so much from you.' And she enabled me to have some hope."

A Shining Example

To me, Mary Aberi epitomizes Attitudinal Healing. She did her utmost to not just think about God but to allow God's light to pour through her for all to behold and partake. She chose not to identify with her body, not to identify with her ego personality. She demonstrated that as long as we are breathing we are here on earth to be a channel for God's blessing, to be centered only on love, and in that way to be of service to others. She somehow knew that death is illusory and that life is eternal. She knew that the mind is not confined to the body and that life and the body are not the same. This was more than a belief with Mary. It was a conviction deep in her heart that inspired conviction in others.

Mary and the others I have spoken of in this book have demonstrated that there is nothing in the material world as important as the love in our hearts. To allow a gradual and ever increasing release of that love is our only function.

May the memory of Mary gently and quietly and frequently remind us that our true mind contains only thoughts of love and peace. All other thoughts we have manufactured ourselves, and therefore we can decide to release them ourselves. This requires no struggle—only the recognition that we would rather have peace than conflict and rather be happy than right. These other thoughts and judgments lead us to believe only what our physical senses tell us has meaning. These thoughts construct around us a world where we are destined to die, a world that is filled with despair, a world in which we are in constant danger of being attacked or abandoned, a world where we are separate from each other and from God. But such a world is not reality.

Let us now choose to forgive the world, to forgive our bodies, and to forgive all those we see. Let us decide to live in the real world of God's love and to have our own internal light shine on everything with a blaze of glory. Let us experience the joy that comes from letting go of our fears, our guilt, our embarrassments, our grievances, and our bitter hopes. Let us be quiet for just an instant and experience the nearness of God, the nearness of boundless and endless love. Let us be still for just one instant and allow God to come to us and bring us back into the center of Love. Let us now have happiness and certainty of purpose. May the unimportant be unimportant forevermore. And may that ancient memory of who and what and where we are rise in our hearts until all this world's pain is gone.

Twenty
Spirituality and God

In this last chapter I want to share with you my sense of my own spiritual journey and relationship with God. At the same time, I also want to make clear that if you were to come to a support group at our Center, it would be rare for you to hear a facilitator using the word *God*. On occasion, a group member might make use of the word, but the Center simply does not promote or employ any religious or spiritual views.

When I founded the Center, I purposely stayed away from using the word *God*. I was still uncomfortable with the word myself, and I rationalized that using it might scare people away. Although it was clear that the focus of our work was to show how practical it is to use spirituality in all aspects of our lives, I didn't feel guided to use the God word. I also didn't want anybody assuming that what we were doing was religious in nature. Letting go of fear has always been one of our aims at the Center, and since many people have hang-ups about God, I felt that any kind of God talk might make people more fearful rather than less.

Even though our work at the Center is spiritual to the very core, the Center is not a religious institution. From the beginning, our doors have been open to people of different religions and no religion, atheists and believers alike. Nor are we theologians. For example, we do not encourage or discourage belief in a Higher Power. We let people know that they are free to choose what to believe and what to put in their minds, and we deliberately avoid trying to change anyone.

That being said, at the Center we also have found that "something" happens within our hearts when we begin to live our lives without judging ourselves or others, when we let go of blame and guilt, and when we love ourselves and the people around us unconditionally.

This "something" is often a sense of spiritual fulfillment and a memory of being joined with all that is alive and with that which created us. For many people this "something" is the memory of God.

Personally, my mind and heart have undergone a deep shift since I wrote the first edition of *Teach Only Love*. My relationship with God is now beyond "belief." I find that I am listening and talking with God all day long. You might say that my day is filled with God talk. My journey from atheist to absolute faith in God required me to forgive certain aspects of my religious training and a few of my early teachers who did not appear to "walk their talk" as well as my own misperceptions of God. Today I do my best to make all decisions based on listening to the inner voice of God and to make my will one with God's will. I now find myself making references to God more frequently in my conversations with others.

When you work with children and adults who are facing death, you begin reevaluating your old beliefs about life and death and about whether there is something greater than us all—a Source that goes by the name of God for many of us. Witnessing numerous people die whom we have come to love has convinced many of us working at the Center that everyone is more than a body and that death is not the end of life. This has made the first principle of Attitudinal Healing, "The essence of our being is love," come alive for us. More and more, our experience has taught us that we are spiritual beings who are just temporarily in bodies.

I don't think that I and the many volunteers at the various Centers for Attitudinal Healing could continue to work with dying patients if we believed that death is the end of life. It would just be too painful. And I have known many people in this field who had no belief that they were on a spiritual journey who did indeed stop working with the dying because it was too painful.

The children, adults, and their families with whom we have worked have become our teachers in every sense of the word. I am reminded that when I was helping to start the original Center in Tiburon, I was an alcoholic. I was afraid to die, yet I was well on the road to drinking myself to death. And I was still vehemently and proudly proclaiming myself an atheist. Yet in my meditation, I was told that these kids were wise old souls in children's bodies teaching me and others spiritual truths and another way of looking at life and death.

Working at the Center opened my heart to a new way of being and living. I grew to know a power far greater than I, a power that I began to call God.

Some years after we started our Center in Tiburon, I had a very significant dream. I was on a plateau at the top of a high mountain, and fifteen of the children I had worked with who had died were with me. We were in a circle going around and around, skipping and dancing, joyful and gleeful. It was one of those dreams that seem to be actually happening and not a dream at all. Suddenly the children released my hands and began floating into the sky, waving happily to me. Then in a most spectacular way, their bodies disappeared and each transformed into a beam of beautiful white light. The whole sky was then filled with light.

For me, the dream meant that each of us is a beam of light, an extension of the radiance of the light of Love that created us. It was a profound reminder that all of us are, indeed, the Light of the World. For me, it was also confirmation that there is no death and that these children and I are joined in Love and Light forever. It was a reminder that we are much more than our physical bodies, that there is a Source guiding us, and that unconditional Love is always here for us.

It has been a wonderful experience for me to see parents come back to the Center after the death of their child to help other parents going through the possibility of their own child dying. A powerful example is Cheryl Shohan, who lost two children from cancer and later developed breast cancer herself. Cheryl now directs the Home and Hospital Visitation Program. There is a light in her that never ceases to shine. That light reflects her tremendous faith in God and her burning desire to continue healing herself by helping others. This she does by using what she learned from her own painful experiences. She gives much hope to parents who believe that they will never be able to feel or live beyond the death of their child.

There are many people I respect and admire who say that they are atheists, yet I experience them as some of the most godly people I know. They are kind, gentle, tender, and compassionate; devoid of judgment; always willing to be helpful to others. *The real issue is not what are our concepts of God but whether we are willing to lead lives in which our hearts are filled with unconditional love, complete forgiveness, and the desire to be truly helpful.*

For me, believing in a loving Source that I call God is comforting and brings peace. I find that it is also helpful to believe that we can direct our will to be one with God's Will and that our thoughts, words, decisions, and actions can be based on the voice of Love rather than the voice of fear. This experience is Oneness and I believe it is what we are all about.

I find myself doing my best to remember God all of the time, in all situations. My trust and faith provide me with joy, with creative energy, and with an inspiration that fills me with bliss and happiness. I now believe that I, like all of us, am on assignment doing God's work, and I can no longer imagine anything that could be more joyful than this.

I know that it is not my function to change people, to attempt to change their beliefs, or to get them to accept God. As I have said before, I believe that we are here to teach only love, and I also believe that we are each the light of the world and that all we are asked is to do our best not to block our light from shining. Another way of expressing this is to say that we each open doors for ourselves and others to examine the choices we make as well as the thoughts and attitudes we put in our minds. In this way we are teacher/student and student/teacher for each other.

It's my personal belief that in the real world of God's Love, there is only Love and nothing else. It is this Love that answers all our problems, questions, conflicts, and suffering. It is what ends the illusion that we are separate from each other and from our Source.

Once again I want to reiterate that at our centers you won't hear much "God talk," but what you will experience is an atmosphere of unconditional love, acceptance, and forgiveness.

EPILOGUE

This poem came to me after my morning meditation and embodies my sense of what Attitudinal Healing is.

WHEN WE TEACH ONLY LOVE

Each of us can make a difference
When we teach only love, not fear
When we put an end to indifference and
When we let go of selfish needs

Each of us can make a difference
When we teach only love
When we awaken each day
By showing each other the way

Each of us can make a difference
When we teach only love
When we commit ourselves to have a heart
That beats only with compassion
Where caring for one another becomes
Our only passion

Each of us can make a difference
When we teach only love
When giving, kindness, patience, gratitude
And tenderness are the way that we pray

When Love and Forgiveness become
Our song of the day
Each of us can make a difference
When we teach only love
When everything we think, say, and do
Becomes our gift of love to God

Each of us can make a difference
When we teach only love
When we commit our lives to joy
When we commit our hearts to peace

Each of us can make a difference
When we teach only love

Other Books by Gerald G. Jampolsky, M.D.

Forgiveness: The Greatest Healer of All

•

Love Is Letting Go of Fear

•

*To Give Is to Receive: An Eighteen Day Mini-Course
on Healing Relationships*

•

*Good-bye to Guilt:
Releasing Fear through Forgiveness*

•

*Out of Darkness into the Light:
A Journey of Inner Healing*

•

*One Person Can Make a Difference:
Ordinary People Doing Extraordinary Things*

With Diane V. Cirincione, Ph.D.

*Love Is the Answer:
Creating Positive Relationships*

*Change Your Mind, Change Your Life:
Concepts in Attitudinal Healing*

•

*"Me First" and the Gimme Gimmes:
A Story of Love and Forgiveness, Choices and Changes*

•

Wake-up Calls

With Lee L. Jampolsky, Ph.D.

*Listen to Me: A Book for Men and Women About
Father-Son Relationships*

Audiocassettes

Love Is Letting Go of Fear

•

Teach Only Love

•

Good-bye to Guilt

•

To Give Is to Receive

•

*Love Is the Answer:
Creating Positive Relationships*

•

Forgiveness Is the Key to Happiness

•

*Introduction to
A Course in Miracles*

•

One Person Can Make a Difference

•

The Quiet Mind

•

Achieving Inner Peace

•

Visions of the Future

•

*Finding the Miracle of Love in Your Life:
Based on A Course in Miracles*

Videocassettes

Achieving Inner and Outer Success

•

Healing Relationships

•

Visions of the Future

For information about the Center for Attitudinal Healing in Sausalito, California, and its workshops, or about other centers, or about the lectures and workshops of Jerry Jampolsky and Diane Cirincione, please contact the Center for Attitudinal Healing, 33 Buchanan Drive, Sausalito, CA 94965; phone: (415) 331-6161; fax: (415) 331-4545, or visit our Web site at www.healingcenter.org.

If you wish to purchase books and audio- or videotapes, please contact Miracle Distributions, 1141 E. Ash Ave., Fullerton, CA 92631; phone: 1-800-359-2246; or contact the Sausalito Center for Attitudinal Healing.

Other Books from
Beyond Words Publishing, Inc.

ADULTS

Forgiveness
The Greatest Healer of All
Author: Gerald G. Jampolsky, M.D.
Foreword: Neale Donald Walsch
$12.95, softcover

Forgiveness: The Greatest Healer of All is written in simple, down-to-earth language. It explains why so many of us find it difficult to forgive and why holding on to grievances is really a decision to suffer. The book describes what causes us to be unforgiving and how our minds work to justify this. It goes on to point out the toxic side effects of being unforgiving and the havoc it can play on our bodies and on our lives. But above all, it leads us to the vast benefits of forgiving. The author shares powerful stories that open our hearts to the miracles which can take place when we truly believe that no one needs to be excluded from our love. Sprinkled throughout the book are Forgiveness Reminders that may be used as daily affirmations supporting a new life free of past grievances.

Healing Your Rift with God
A Guide to Spiritual Renewal and Ultimate Healing
Author: Paul Sibcy
$14.95, softcover

God, says Paul Sibcy, is everything that is. All of us—faithful seekers or otherwise—have some area of confusion, hurt, or denial around this word, or our personal concept of God, that keeps us from a full expression of our spirituality. *Healing Your Rift with God* is a guidebook for finding our own personal rifts with God and healing them. Sibcy explains the nature of a spiritual rift, how this wound can impair our lives, and how such a wound may be healed by the earnest seeker, with or without help from a counselor or teacher. *Healing Your Rift with God* will also assist those in the helping professions who wish to facilitate what the author calls ultimate healing. The book includes many personal stories from the author's life, teaching, and counseling work, and its warm narrative tone creates an intimate author–reader relationship that inspires the healing process.

Rites of Passage
Celebrating Life's Changes
Authors: Kathleen Wall, Ph.D., and Gary Ferguson
$12.95, softcover

Every major transition in our lives—be it marriage, high-school graduation, the death of a parent or spouse, or the last child leaving home—brings with it opportunities for growth and self-actualization and for repositioning ourselves in the world. Personal ritual—the focus of *Rites of Passage*—allows us to use the energy held within the anxiety of change to nourish the new person that is forever struggling to be born. *Rites of Passage* begins by explaining to readers that human growth is not linear, as many of us assume, but rather occurs in a five-part cycle. After sharing the patterns of transition, the authors then show the reader how ritual can help him or her move through these specific life changes: work and career, intimate relationships, friends, divorce, changes within the family, adolescence, issues in the last half of life, and personal loss.

The Great Wing
A Parable
Author: Louis A. Tartaglia, M.D.; Foreword: Father Angelo Scolozzi
$14.95, hardcover

The Great Wing transforms the timeless miracle of the migration of a flock of geese into a parable for the modern age. It recounts a young goose's own reluctant but steady transformation from gangly fledgling to Grand Goose and his triumph over the turmoils of his soul and the buffeting of a mighty Atlantic storm. In *The Great Wing*, our potential as individuals is affirmed, as is the power of group prayer, or the "Flock Mind." As we make the journey with this goose and his flock, we rediscover that we tie our own potential into the power of the common good by way of attributes such as honesty, hope, courage, trust, perseverance, spirituality, and service. The young goose's trials and tribulations, as well as his triumph, are our own.

Watermelon Magic
Seeds of Wisdom, Slices of Life
Author: Wally Amos
$14.95, softcover

Watermelon Magic is an inspirational/motivational book using watermelons as a metaphor for life. Utilizing the life experiences of Wally Amos, the book shows the parallels between watermelons and humans. *Watermelon Magic* tells how Wally Amos uses his faith in everyday life and the wisdom gained from the past to help him make wise choices. Just as the vine connects the watermelons, we are all connected by spirit. And just as prickly vines make it difficult to get the melons, our human connections are sometimes prickly, making it difficult for us to achieve our goals and realize our dreams. *Watemelon Magic* helps us acknowledge the difficulties and choose a path to success.

Nurturing Your Child with Music
How Sound Awareness Creates Happy, Smart, and Confident Children
Author: John M. Ortiz, Ph.D.
$14.95, softcover

Author and psychomusicologist Dr. John Ortiz says that we have "just begun to tap into the powers behind the timeless element of sound," and in his book *Nurturing Your Child with Music*, Dr. Ortiz allows the reader to discover those musical powers through and with their children. Designed for parents who take an active inter-est in their children's lives, this book offers a number of creative methods through which families can initiate, enhance, and main-tain happy, relaxed, and productive home environments. *Nurturing Your Child with Music* includes easy-to-do exercises and fun activi-ties to bring music and sound into parenting styles and family life. The book provides music menus and sample "days of sound" to use during the prenatal, newborn, preschool, and school-age phases.

Dr. Ortiz shares how we can keep our family "in tune" and create harmony in our homes by inviting music and sound into our daily dance of life.

Discovering Another Way
Raising Brighter Children While Having a Meaningful Career
Author: Lane Nemeth
$16.95, softcover

Discovery Toys is a pioneer in the educational toy market. In *Discovering Another Way*, founder Lane Nemeth tells how she built this $100 million company from the ground up, a company that helped change the lives of tens of thousands of women and an entire generation of kids who have grown up smarter in "Discovery Toys Families." The book provides a refreshingly candid insider's view of how to start your own business *and* follow your heart, enriching your children's minds and imaginations *at the same time*. It is also a heartwarming story of Lane Nemeth's dedication to bring quality toys that spark a sense of discovery and learning to all children, not just a chosen few. Interspersed throughout Lane's story are chapters revealing the gems of parenting wisdom she discovered while raising her family *and* her business: "So You Want a Cooperative Child?," "Guidelines for Brain-Building Play," "How to Turn Your Child into a Lifelong Reader," and "Five Ways to Enhance Your Time with Your Child." Lane explains the magic of learning moments and shows parents how to turn every occasion into an opportunity for discovery and learning.

Nurturing Spirituality in Children
Author: Peggy J. Jenkins, Ph.D.
$12.95, softcover

Children who develop a healthy balance of mind and spirit enter adulthood with high self-esteem, better able to respond to life's challenges. Many parents wish to heighten their children's spiritual awareness but have been unable to find good resources. *Nurturing Spirituality in Children* offers scores of simple lessons that parents can teach to their children in less than ten minutes at a time.

Questions for My Father
Finding the Man Behind Your Dad
Author: Vin Staniforth
$15.00, hardcover

Questions for My Father is a little book that asks big questions—some serious, some playful, some risky. Each question is an opportunity to open, rejuvenate, or bring closure to the powerful but often overlooked relationship between fathers and children. Fathers have long been regarded as objects of mystery and fascination. *Questions for My Father* provides a blueprint for uncovering the full dimensions of the man behind the mystery. It offers a way to let fathers tell their personal stories and to let children explore their own knowledge and understanding of one of the largest figures in their lives. In rediscovering their dad, readers will discover themselves.

A Guy's Guide to Pregnancy
Preparing for Parenthood Together
Author: Frank Mungeam; Foreword: John Gray, Ph.D.
$12.95, softcover

Every day, four thousand American men become first-time dads. There are literally hundreds of pregnancy guidebooks aimed at women, but guys rarely rate more than a footnote. *A Guy's Guide to Pregnancy* is the first book to explain in "guy terms" the changes that happen to a man's partner and their relationship during pregnancy, using a humorous yet insightful approach. Future fathers will find out what to expect when they enter the "Pregnancy Zone." *A Guy's Guide to Pregnancy* is designed to be guy-friendly—approachable in appearance as well as content and length. It is divided into forty brisk chapters, one for each week of the pregnancy.

The Intuitive Way
A Guide to Living from Inner Wisdom
Author: Penney Peirce; Foreword: Carol Adrienne
$16.95, softcover

When intuition is in full bloom, life takes on a magical, effortless quality; your world is suddenly full of synchronicities, creative insights, and abundant knowledge just for the asking. *The Intuitive*

Way shows you how to enter that state of perceptual aliveness and integrate it into daily life to achieve greater natural flow through an easy-to-understand, ten-step course. Author Penney Peirce synthesizes teachings from psychology, East-West philosophy, religion, metaphysics, and business. In simple and direct language, Peirce describes the intuitive process as a new way of life and demonstrates many practical applications from speeding decision-making to expanding personal growth. Whether you're just beginning to search for a richer, fuller life experience or are looking for more subtle, sophisticated insights about your spiritual path, *The Intuitive Way* will be your companion as you progress through the stages of intuition development.

The Woman's Book of Dreams
Dreaming as a Spiritual Practice
Author: Connie Cockrell Kaplan; Foreword: Jamie Sams
$14.95, softcover

Dreams are the windows to your future and the catalysts to bringing the new and creative into your life. Everyone dreams. Understanding the power of dreaming helps you achieve your greatest potential with ease. *The Woman's Book of Dreams* emphasizes the uniqueness of women's dreaming and shows the reader how to dream with intention, clarity, and focus. In addition, this book will teach you how to recognize the thirteen types of dreams, how your monthly cycles affect your dreaming, how the moon's position in the sky and its relationship to your astrological chart determine your dreaming, and how to track your dreams and create a personal map of your dreaming patterns. Connie Kaplan guides you through an ancient woman's group form called dream circle—a sacred space in which to share dreams with others on a regular basis. Dream circle allows you to experience life's mystery by connecting with other dreamers. It shows you that through dreaming together with your circle, you create the reality in which you live. It is time for you to recognize the power of dreams and to put yours into action. This book will inspire you to do all that—and more.

The Second Wives Club
Secrets for Becoming Lovers for Life
Authors: Lenore Fogelson Millian, Ph.D., and
Stephen Jerry Millian, Ph.D.
$14.95, softcover

Are you or someone you know a second wife? Are you tired of arguing about your husband's first marriage? *The Second Wives Club* is the book you've been waiting for. Join the Club and learn the six secrets of successful second marriages. Learn how you can have wedded bliss while avoiding the pitfalls that second marriages bring. Don't be put off by his ex-wife. Help him get rid of his old "baggage" and make space in your relationship to be lovers for life. Includes chapters on how to deal with the first wife, the children, the grandchildren, the mother-in-law, the friends, and the memories.

Create Your Own Love Story
The Art of Lasting Relationships
Author: David W. McMillan, Ph.D.; Foreword: John Gray, Ph.D.
$21.95, hardcover; $14.95, softcover

Create Your Own Love Story breaks new ground in the crowded and popular field of relationship self-help guides. *Create Your Own Love Story* is based on a four-part model—Spirit, Trust, Trade, and Art—derived from McMillan's twenty years' work in community theory and clinical psychology. Each of these four elements is divided into short, highly readable chapters that include both touching and hilarious examples from real marriages, brief exercises based on visualization and journal writing that are effective whether used by one or both partners, and dialogues readers can have with themselves and/or their partners. This book shows readers how they can use their own energy and initiative, with McMillan's help, to make their marriage stronger, more enduring, and more soul-satisfying.

Love Sweeter Love
Creating Relationships of Simplicity and Spirit
Author: Jann Mitchell; Foreword: Súsan Jeffers
$12.95, softcover

How do we find the time to nurture relationships with the people we love? By simplifying. And *Love Sweeter Love* teaches us how to decide who and what is most important, how to work together as a couple, and how to savor life's sweetest moments. Mitchell has warm, practical, easy-to-understand advice for everyone—young, mature, single, married, or divorced—interested in creating simple, sacred time for love.

Home Sweeter Home
Creating a Haven of Simplicity and Spirit
Author: Jann Mitchell; Foreword: Jack Canfield
$12.95, softcover

We search the world for spirituality and peace—only to discover that happiness and satisfaction are not found "out there" in the world but right here in our houses and in our hearts. Award-winning journalist and author Jann Mitchell offers creative insights and suggestions for making our home life more nurturing, spiritual, and rewarding for ourselves, our families, and our friends.

CHILDREN'S

She Is Born
A Celebration of Daughters
Author: Virginia Kroll; Illustrator: John Rowe
$15.95, hardcover

She Is Born is a moving tribute to a girl's birth and growth, beginning with a clap of thunder as the words "she is born" echo across the Earth and ending with the possibility of that girl becoming a mother herself one day. The story shows how cultures around the world welcome and celebrate the birth of a daughter. The author and illustrator's painstaking research ensures that all of the book's cultural details are genuine and accurate. The rituals, celebrations, and traditions are described in poetic detail, conveying the sense of wonder and pride accompanying a daughter's birth.

When Woman Became the Sea
A Costa Rican Creation Myth
Author: Susan Strauss; Illustrator: Cristina Acosta
$14.95, hardcover

When Woman Became the Sea is one culture's beautiful explanation of how the world began. It will provide a strong example of an inspiring female heroine who joins with the gods in creation. This book is illustrated by Cristina Acosta, a Hispanic artist, who has wonderfully captured the essence of her culture. A sense of joyous energy and movement defines her bright, whimsical paintings. Children will love learning about the culture of exotic Costa Rica, and they will enjoy this explanation of the origin of the sea.

The Time of the Lion
Author: Caroline Pitcher; Illustrator: Jackie Morris
$15.95, hardcover

This touching father/son tale explores an unusual friendship and a child's rite of passage. *The Time of the Lion* creates a metaphor for the magic of childhood, a time when fantasy is reality and lions are our friends. The beautiful artwork is the perfect complement to this tale, capturing the power and mystery of the African savannah. Let it always be the Time of the Lion.

Imagine
Author/illustrator: Bart Vivian
$14.95, hardcover

"If you can imagine things aren't quite what they seem, and dream of possibilities that only you can dream of, then anything can happen." And so begins the inspiring, poetic book *Imagine*, a celebration of the wonder and innocence of childhood. In a playful back-and-forth, *Imagine* asks readers to imagine ordinary, everyday events as wondrous and magical occurrences. The everyday scenes of childhood are illustrated in luxurious black-and-white, while the magical settings are in full, vibrant color. Readers of *Imagine* will be inspired to explore adventures in their minds. For children, the book is a touchstone for engaging their wonderfully creative minds. For parents and grandparents, it's an opportunity to look back to a simpler time in their own lives, a time filled with endless possibilities.

Turtle Songs
A Tale for Mothers and Daughters
Author: Margaret Wolfson; Illustrator: Karla Sachi
$14.95, hardcover
There are, within the world's cultures, ancient myths that are told over centuries of time. Occasionally, these stories take on a life of their own and speak to people everywhere. *Turtle Songs*, from the island of Kadavu in Fiji, is such a story. So great is the influence of this tale, that to this day on Kadavu, women sing ancient songs in tribute to the Turtle Princess, as they stand on cliffs over the sea. As the women sing, enormous sea turtles rise from the depths of the ocean in response to the songs. Such is the magic of this story. All great stories are meant to be told, and now *Turtle Songs* has been brought from the mists of Fiji to daughters, mothers, and dreamers everywhere.

Girls Know Best
Advice for Girls from Girls on Just About Everything
Editor: Michelle Roehm
$8.95, softcover
Girls Know Best contains the writings of thirty-eight different girls from across the United States. The book is divided into chapters focusing on specific issues and giving advice from the girl writers to the girl readers. The topics include living with siblings, school/homework, parents, divorce, and dealing with stepfamilies, boys, friends, losses when your best friend moves away or you do, depression, dealing with differences (race and religion), drugs, our bodies and looks, and overcoming life's biggest obstacles. Each writing includes a photo of the girl author and a brief background about her and her dreams. Breaking up these chapters are fun activities that girls can do together or by themselves, including best-friend crafts, ways kids can save the environment, ideas for volunteering, natural beauty fun, and even how to pass notes in class without getting caught. The book is a vehicle for encouraging

girls to use their creativity and to believe in themselves and their infinite potential. By showing that any girl can do it, our girl authors will be models and inspirations for all girls.

Girls Know Best 2
Tips on Life and Fun Stuff to Do
Editor: Marianne Monson-Burton; Introduction: Tara Lipinski
$8.95, softcover

Girls Know Best 2 builds upon the success of *Girls Know Best*, but it has developed its own personality with unique new chapter ideas and forty-seven new girl authors from across the country. These amazing girls have written chapters giving advice on things like shyness, the Internet, making money, and slumber parties. They've also written chapters with fun activities like how to analyze your dreams, redecorate your room, and even the best way to survive grounding! Everything you need to know from the people who really know the answers—girls just like you!

Girls Know Best 3
Your Words, Your World
Editor: Marianne Monson-Burton; Introduction: Picabo Street
$8.95, softcover

The girls of America asked for it, and here it is—*Girls Know Best 3*—the latest book in the only advice series written by girls for girls. Incredible chapters by new authors ages seven to sixteen were chosen from a nationwide writing contest. Girls offer advice on topics like trying out for sports, gaining confidence, and keeping pen pals. You will also find out about great activities such as starting clubs, doing art projects, and joining a band! With *Girls Know Best 3*, we are proud to continue the tradition of great advice and activity books real girls can count on because they are written by girls just like them.

Boys Know It All
Wise Thoughts and Wacky Ideas from Guys Like You
Editor: Michelle Roehm
$8.95, softcover

Stereotypes and the pressure to conform often smother the creativity of boys and leave their fresh, original ideas unheard. *Boys Know It All* is a place where boys can speak their piece about what it is to be a boy. Boys, ages six to sixteen, have written chapters offering helpful hints for tough situations like talking to girls and surviving older siblings, while others toss out ways to fill free time creatively like inventing your own family traditions and taking care of pets. This is a fun book that also tackles serious issues about growing up male in America. Boys will enjoy reading it and will even get excited about learning and trying new things.

Girls Who Rocked the World
Heroines from Sacagawea to Sheryl Swoopes
Author: Amelie Welden
$8.95, softcover

Girls Who Rocked the World, a companion book to the *Girls Know Best* series, encourages girls to believe in themselves and go for their dreams. It tells the stories of thirty-five real girls, past and present, from all around the world, who achieved amazing feats and changed history before reaching their twenties. Included are well-known girls like Helen Keller and Sacagawea as well as many often-overlooked heroines such as Joan of Arc, Phillis Wheatley, and Wang Yani. Interspersed along with the stories of heroines are photos and writings of real girls from all over America answering the question, "How do I plan to rock the world?" By highlighting the goals and dreams of these girls, the book links these historical heroines to girls today who will be the next ones to rock the world!

So, You Wanna Be A Rock Star?
Author: Stephen Anderson; Introduction: Eric Stefani
$8.95, softcover

A hip, how-to book that teaches young, aspiring musicians how to achieve their rock-and-roll dreams. The book begins with the basics, telling kids how to start their own bands with only their friends, a set of drums, and a lot of inspiration. In a fun yet informative style, Anderson teaches kids how to practice, get gigs in public, and maybe even become famous! The book contains both practical advice and cool insights into how real bands get discovered. *So, You Wanna Be A Rock Star?* also profiles twenty real kids who are out there right now, accomplishing their dreams by practicing and performing in public. By highlighting the real-life rock successes of everyday kids, the book sends the message that if you believe in yourself, anything can happen!

To order or to request a catalog, contact
Beyond Words Publishing, Inc.
20827 N.W. Cornell Road, Suite 500
Hillsboro, OR 97124-9808
503-531-8700 or 1-800-284-9673

You can also visit our Web site at *www.beyondword.com* or e-mail us at *info@beyondword.com*.

Beyond Words Publishing, Inc.

Our Corporate Mission:

Inspire to Integrity

Our Declared Values:

We give to all of life as life has given us.
We honor all relationships.
Trust and stewardship are integral to fulfilling dreams.
Collaboration is essential to create miracles.
Creativity and aesthetics nourish the soul.
Unlimited thinking is fundamental.
Living your passion is vital.
Joy and humor open our hearts to growth.
It is important to remind ourselves of love.